THE KID'S GUIDE TO SERVICE PROJECTS

Over 500 Service Ideas for Young People Who Want to Make a Difference

Barbara A. Lewis

author of *The Kid's Guide to Social Action,*
Kids with Courage, and *What Do You Stand For?*

Edited by Pamela Espeland

free spirit
PUBLiSHiNG®

Works
for kids™

P9-DVV-215

Library of Congress Cataloging-in-Publication Data
Lewis, Barbara A., 1943–
    The kid's guide to service projects : over 500 service ideas for young
people who want to make a difference / Barbara A. Lewis ; edited by
Pamela Espeland.
        p.   cm.
    Includes index.
    Summary: Describes a variety of opportunities for youngsters to
participate in successful community service.
    ISBN 0-915793-82-2
    1. Student volunteers in social service—United States—Juvenile
literature. 2. Student service—United States—Juvenile literature.
    [1. Student service. 2. Volunteer workers in social service.]
    I. Espeland, Pamela, 1951–   . II. Title.
    HV41.L455   1995
    361.3'7'0835—dc20   94-47933
                                                                      CIP
                                                                       AC

10 9 8 7 6
Printed in the United States of America

Cover and book design by MacLean & Tuminelly
Index compiled by Theresa Wolner and Eileen Quam

Free Spirit Publishing Inc.
400 First Avenue North, Suite 616
Minneapolis, MN 55401
(612) 338-2068

Dedication

To all of you who desire to serve:
"...ask not what your country can do for you;
ask what you can do for your country."
John Fitzgerald Kennedy

This book is dedicated to Mike,
who makes service a habit.

Acknowledgments

I would like to acknowledge my publisher, Judy Galbraith, and my editor, Pamela Espeland, for their honesty; their caring, creative ideas, support, and friendship; and their idealism.

Thanks to Daphne Williams, Volunteer Specialist for Salt Lake City School District, for sharing her ideas and for first giving me a broader vision of what volunteerism is.

A special recognition to all the students I have been associated with at Jackson Elementary—those who have creatively and tirelessly volunteered in the school and community in cleaning up hazardous waste, working for sidewalk repairs, planting trees, and fighting crime.

Thanks to my principals, Peter Gallegos and Marilyn Phillips, Superintendent John Bennion, the Salt Lake City School District, and State Office of Education for their support.

I would like to acknowledge The United Way, The American Newspaper Publishers Association Foundation, and the Peanuts Gang for their "Cheers for Volunteers," from which I gleaned a few ideas including the idea to "trim a mitten tree."

Thanks to my family members for their continued, relentless support and love: Larry, my dear husband and best friend, and my wonderful children: Mike, Andrea, Christian, and Sam.

And finally, thanks to my dear friends, Jetta and Kathy, who continue to make it possible for me to have time to write.

Contents

Introduction

When a class of sixth graders in Utah discovered a neighborhood toxic waste site, they decided to do something about it. Their efforts led to the cleanup of the site and a state Superfund for cleaning up other hazardous waste in their state.

A Florida teenager began a project to feed the hungry every Thanksgiving.

Kids in Texas banded together to save a historic battleship from the scrap heap.

A Georgia 16-year-old saved a historic courthouse from the wrecking ball.

A teenager in Pennsylvania started a town library.

A California 12-year-old began helping young crime victims.

Across the United States and around the world, tens of thousands of young people are making a difference in their neighborhoods, schools, and communities. They're collecting cans for food shelves, reading to seniors, recycling, and planting trees. They're working alone and in groups to identify problems and come up with solutions.

If they can do it, so can you.

Maybe you're thinking, "I'm just one person!" So what? Lots of young people serve others on their own. Or they start on their own and inspire others to join them.

Maybe you're telling yourself, "This sounds interesting, but I'm already too busy and I don't have the time." Wrong! Many young people involved in service projects keep up with their school work, have jobs, get together with their friends, do chores at home, take part in school activities, and still have time to reach out and help others.

Maybe you're wondering, "What could I do?" Keep reading! This book is full of ideas for you to try.

How to Use This Book

The Kid's Guide to Service Projects contains more than 500 ideas for service for young people of all ages. They range from simple projects (running an errand for a friend) to complex projects (working for a state law to create stronger penalties against graffiti).

Start by scanning the contents. What interests you? The environment? Politics? Helping homeless people? Safety? Animals? Fighting crime? Literacy? If you pick an area that appeals to you personally, you'll have more fun, and you'll be more likely to stay committed and get the job done.

Once you choose your area, turn to that part of the book and skim through the ideas. Pick one that catches your eye. Then go to "Ten Steps to Successful Service Projects" on pages 7–12. You'll learn how to get started, get the help you need, and evaluate your experience.

What if you don't find *the* idea that makes you want to get involved? Then use this book as a starting-point for brainstorming your own ideas. Don't forget to check with your school, scout troop, community group, or faith community. People there will have many suggestions for service projects.

What's In It for You?

Why should you get involved in a service project? You may already know at least one answer to that question: Because it's the right thing to do.

If you're tired of seeing trash on your streets, if the thought of people going hungry drives you crazy, if you're worried about the world you're about to inherit, then it's obvious to you that *someone* has to do *something*. You can be that someone, even if you're "just a kid."

If you're as sick as I am of the media reports of kids who cause trouble—as gang members, drug users, vandals, and violent criminals—then you'll welcome the chance to prove that young people can be a powerful force for positive change.

If you're worried that your community is becoming an unsafe place to live, work, and play, you can help to turn it around. A service project is a great way to bring people together. When people come together, neighborhoods are stronger. People start watching out for one another. Friendships form. Maybe your neighbor across the street, across the hall, or across the alley has ideas and skills to contribute to your project. Ask!

Imagine how good it will feel to know that your actions are making a difference in people's lives. Your self-esteem will soar, and you'll gain new confidence. Along the way, you'll develop new talents and abilities—leadership skills, organizational skills, public speaking skills, and more.

As you apply to colleges and look for jobs, you'll discover that admissions officials and employers are impressed by young people who serve. More and more colleges are looking beyond grades and test scores for students who give of themselves. More and more companies are encouraging their employees to contribute their time and energy to community service projects.

You might even find your life's direction. Many young people are concerned or confused about what the future might bring. They don't know what they want to be or become, often because they have little or no experience beyond the usual—family, friends, school. A service project can put you in touch with people you might not otherwise meet and opportunities you might not otherwise have. Your personal world will expand and grow in ways you never imagined.

You'll feel *yourself* growing in positive—and surprising—ways. Service gives us the chance to break down our preconceived notions and prejudices. Do you think that people are poor because they're lazy? Just wait until you get to know someone who happens to be poor. Do you believe that elderly people have little to offer you? You can develop new friendships. Do you sometimes have a hard time getting along with people of other races? Tensions tend to fade when people work side-by-side or reach out to one another.

As you get involved in your service project, you may want to keep a journal. Write down the things you do for the project you've chosen...and write down what your project does for *you*. Record your feelings, experiences, and insights. At the end, you might describe how you have changed. Because you *will have* changed. You can count on it.

Imagine the Possibilities

According to the U.S. Bureau of the Census, there were 46,654,000 kids ages 5–17 in the United States in 1992. Add to that another 29,667,000 young people ages 18–25. What would happen if all 76 million decided to start serving their communities?

Government solutions to society's problems and needs are slow and expensive. Young people are able to cut through red tape and get results while adults are still wondering where to start.

What gives you this amazing ability? Unlike adults, you don't know ahead of time all the reasons why something might *not* work! Instead of making excuses, you take action. You've got the clout—and the numbers—to bring about major social changes.

Will Service Become a Requirement?

On November 16, 1990, President George Bush signed into law the National Community Service Act, which set aside about $62 million to encourage young people to serve their communities and schools. This amount has been increased each year since then. Schools across the country are setting up service experiences for students of all ages. Many high schools, both public and private, are making service a requirement for graduation.

But even if service becomes a requirement in your school, I hope you won't perceive it as something other people are forcing you to do. Then service becomes just another obligation—a chore. Instead, let yourself approach it with enthusiasm and dedication. Throw yourself into it. Get excited...even passionate. Then the requirement becomes secondary, the credit or school evaluation unimportant, because you're doing it for *yourself*.

I Want to Hear from You

If you choose a service project from this book—or if you use this book to brainstorm your own idea—I want to hear from you. Write to me and tell me about your project. What did you want to accomplish? How did you go about doing it? How did your efforts make a difference? How did your project change someone else's life? How did it change your life?

I have so much confidence in young people today. I know for a fact that kids can accomplish incredible things. I see it every year in my own classroom, with my own students. And I'm eager to hear it from you. You can write to me at this address:

Barbara A. Lewis
c/o Free Spirit Publishing Inc.
400 First Avenue North, Suite 616
Minneapolis, MN 55401-1730

I look forward to reading your story.

Barbara A. Lewis

TEN STEPS TO SUCCESSFUL SERVICE PROJECTS

1. Research your project.

Choose an issue that concerns you, then come up with a project related to that issue. Consider these questions:

- What would I like to do?

- What might benefit the most people?

- What might make the biggest difference?

- What can I afford (in terms of time, money, etc.)?

- What is really possible for me to do?

- What _____? (Add your own questions.)

2. Form a team.

If you don't want to go it alone, or if the project seems too complicated to do by yourself, invite others to join you.

- Choose people who share your interest in the project and who are likely to stay with you until it is completed.

- Look around at your family, friends, school, neighborhood, community, or faith community for possibilities.

- Don't limit your group to people your own age. Invite younger kids to get involved. See if college students and seniors in your area want to help.

3. Find a sponsor.

Ask a responsible adult (teacher, parent, neighbor, scout leader, etc.) to act as your sponsor. This can give your project credibility with other adults whose help and/or permission you might need.

4. Make a plan.

■ Decide when and where to meet. You'll want to meet frequently to discuss your project, decide who will do what, identify any problems, and report on your progress.

■ Decide how you will get to the meeting place and service location. Will you need cars, buses, adult drivers? You might need permission slips from your parents. Can you walk or bike there?

■ Define your goal. What do you hope to achieve?

■ Set a schedule. How long will your project take? How much time will you spend each week on your project? When is the date you want to be finished with your project?

■ Estimate your costs. How much money will you need? Make a list of everything you can think of that might or will cost money. What about transportation? Materials? Equipment? Supplies? Photocopying? Postage? Donations? What else?

■ Think hard about your project. Is it realistic? Is it too complicated? Too simple? How could you improve it?

5. Consider the recipient.

Make sure that the people you plan to serve really want your help. What's the best way to do this? Ask! Then find out as much about them as you can. For example:

■ What are their needs? (They may be different than you think, and you may need to revise your plan accordingly.)

■ When are they available? During what hours on what days?

■ Are there any limitations or restrictions? What about special diets? Physical limitations? Allergies? Other health issues?

6. Decide where you will perform your service.

Will you go to the people you plan to serve, or will they come to you?

■ If you go to them, be sure to visit the location ahead of time. Is there enough room to do your project? Does the location have everything you will need? If not, what will you have to bring? How will you get it there? Will you have a place to store things?

■ If they come to you, make sure that your location has what you need.

7. Get any permissions you need to proceed.

Depending on your project, you might need to get permission from:

■ your principal

■ your teacher(s)

■ school district personnel

■ your youth leader

■ your parents

■ your neighbors

■ community organizations

■ owners of any facilities you will want to use

■ anyone else?

8. Advertise.

Let other people know about your project.

- Make a one-page flier (see pages 152–153).

- Or create a public service announcement (see pages 158–159).

- Or send out a press release (see pages 154–155).

9. Fundraise.

Do you need startup money for your service project? Will you need to buy equipment or supplies? If you need to print 150 fliers at your local print shop, who will pay for the printing? If your project will cost anything beyond pocket money, you'll need to fundraise (see pages 167–169).

10. When your project has ended, evaluate it.

Reflect on your experience. Discuss it with your team, family, teachers, friends, and neighbors. Talk it over with the people you served. Describe it in a journal. Write a poem, story, essay, or play about it; create music, dance, or art about it; make a video or tape recording. Try to address questions like:

- What did you learn?

- What did you accomplish?

- What were your feelings, fears, joys?

- Would you do it again?

- How could you improve it?

- Will you repeat it? When? How soon? (You might use your poem, story, essay, play, video, etc. to inspire others to join you.)

Find Out More

There are many groups and organizations that promote youth service. Here are three you can contact for information and assistance.

Corporation for National Service
1100 Vermont Avenue, NW
Eleventh Floor
Washington, DC 20525
(202) 606-5000

Provides information on service learning projects and state directors for youth service.

NYLC (National Youth Leadership Council)
1910 West County Road B
Roseville, MN 55113
(612) 631-3672

The clearinghouse for Serve America offers information, projects, materials, training, and technical assistance for service learning.

Youth Service America
1101 15th Street, NW
Washington, DC 20005
(202) 296-2992

Promotes youth service programs and offers technical assistance.

ANIMALS

Control Animal Populations

There are tens of thousands of stray animals in our towns and cities. Some have been abandoned. Others have been born to homeless strays. Most are starving, sick, and scared. If you care about animals, you can help.

■ Telephone or write to your local humane society or animal shelter to get the latest statistics on the numbers of homeless dogs and cats in your community. Ask their advice on what needs to be done.

■ Start an information campaign.

▷ Create a flier describing the problem of too many stray animals (see pages 152–153).

▷ Distribute it to schools.

▷ Post it in storefronts and grocery stores around your community.

■ Write a proposal for a Free Spaying or Neutering Day (see page 157). Present it to an animal shelter.

▷ Plan the event for a low-income area where people might not be able to afford to have their pets spayed or neutered.

▷ Offer a pet pick-up and return service.

■ Start a petition for controlling your local pet population (see pages 153–154).

   ▷ When you have collected many signatures, present your petition to your mayor or city/town council.

Adopt a Zoo Animal

Zoos are expensive to run. It costs money to buy animals, give them safe, comfortable housing, feed them properly, and provide them with medical care. For most zoos, those costs are not covered by admission fees. The zoos—and the animals— depend on donations and volunteers. If you enjoy visiting your local zoo, you can help by adopting an animal.

■ Telephone your local zoo and ask which animals need help. Find out what the animals need the most. Examples:

   ▷ better habitats

   ▷ more animals (is the lion lonely? does the zoo have a breeding program, and does a monkey need a mate?)

   ▷ medicines

▷ supplies

▷ food

▷ more zoo workers (are there enough workers to give the animals the care they need?).

■ Adopt an animal from an endangered species.

▷ Call local radio and television stations to tell them about your adoption. They may feature your story and inspire other people to adopt endangered animals.

■ Volunteer to help with your adopted animal. You might be able to:

▷ clean habitats and pens

▷ remodel habitats or build new ones

▷ help with feeding

▷ help with a telephone fundraising campaign

▷ help with a public information campaign

▷ distribute fliers.

More Ideas for Helping Animals

■ Find homes in shelters for abandoned pets.

■ Initiate or support a city ordinance to help homeless animals (see pages 163–164).

■ Find out what birds are in your neighborhood.
   ▷ Research what they eat and need.
   ▷ Set out food and water for them.
   ▷ Provide them with shelter.

■ Join a wildlife organization. Be an active member.

■ Care for a neighbor's pet.

■ Visit an animal research facility where they experiment on animals to find cures for diseases. Decide how you feel about this issue.

■ Start a Pet Lovers' Club. Invite others to join.
   ▷ Have special presentations on caring for pets, obedience training, playing with pets, pet grooming, etc.
   ▷ Your club could volunteer at the local humane society—a good place to find new pets.

If You Love Animals...

The American Society for the Prevention of Cruelty to Animals provides educational materials on the humane treatment of animals. Write or call:

> ASPCA (American Society for the Prevention of Cruelty to Animals)
> Education Department
> 424 East 92nd Street
> New York, NY 10128
> (212) 876-7700

COMMUNITY DEVELOPMENT AND BEAUTIFICATION

Neighborhood Building Blocks

When you walk around your city or neighborhood, do you see any vacant lots, clutter, abandoned houses, or other conditions which cause you to raise your eyebrows? Perhaps you're in a small community and your library doesn't have enough books to suit you, or there aren't enough trees. Or maybe there isn't a satisfactory place for young people to shoot a few baskets or ride bikes. You can do more than wonder at these conditions. You might be able to do something to improve your community. And you would be in the company of thousands of young people across the nation who are painting houses, recycling litter, and even establishing branches of libraries.

- Regularly remove debris from anyplace where it seems to collect.

- Clean up a vacant lot.

- Write a proposal to your city or town asking that a vacant lot be turned into a playground (see page 157).

  ▷ Apply for city funds to develop your playground.

- Write letters to support or oppose the development of a plot of land in your neighborhood.

- Paint fences.

▷ Repair fences.

▷ Place fences where they can improve public safety.

■ Start a petition for placing a streetlight or crosswalk at a dangerous intersection (see pages 153–154).

▷ When you have collected many signatures, present your petition to city officials.

■ Identify corners where bushes and trees make it difficult for drivers to see.

▷ If they are on private property, offer to help trim them.

▷ If they are on public property, contact city officials and ask that they be trimmed.

■ Renovate an abandoned house.

▷ Use it as a library.

▷ Use it as an after-school recreation facility.

■ Plant trees, flowers, and other vegetation in vacant spots around your neighborhood.

▷ Plant around your clubhouse.

▷ Plant around your school.

■ Clean up a stream bed.

▷ Plant vegetation along its banks. (Check with local parks officials first.)

■ Help an elderly neighbor.

▷ Mow the lawn.

▷ Pull the weeds.

▷ Shovel the snow.

▷ Paint the fence.

▷ Do whatever needs to be done.

■ Hold a paint-a-thon to help senior citizens, low-income residents, and people with special needs. Work with friends, neighbors, and other volunteers to paint and repair their houses.

■ Write a proclamation for a Neighborhood Beautification Week (see pages 155–156).

> ▷ Ask your mayor or city council member to sign your proclamation.

> ▷ Make copies of your proclamation and distribute them to local businesses and community organizations.

■ Join or organize a campaign to place a decorative fountain in a public place.

■ Petition your city for more drinking fountains and/or restrooms in public areas (see pages 153–154).

■ Start your own neighborhood community council if one doesn't exist.

> ▷ You could sit on an adult council or start your own youth neighborhood council.

> ▷ Work with your local council, local government, or school.

■ Make your neighborhood safer and more welcoming for people with special needs.

> ▷ Interview people with special needs to find out their ideas.

> ▷ One important issue is the accessibility of public places. Are sidewalk curbs cut so people in wheelchairs can cross streets? Do public buildings have ramps? Is handicapped parking available? Are public restrooms accessible and equipped for people with special needs?

> ▷ Petition your city or community for solutions to problems you find (see pages 153–154).

■ Write stories about the history of your city or neighborhood for your community newspaper.

> ▷ Or produce your own community newspaper.

More Ideas for Improving Your Community

■ Conduct a neighborhood drive to collect used furniture.

▷ Distribute it to immigrant families and low-income families.

▷ Bring it to shelters and community organizations.

■ Create a flier highlighting the special attractions of your city or state (see pages 152–153).

▷ Distribute it through your local tourist bureau.

■ Get training to be a guide or host for city tours.

■ Make maps of local parks, libraries, or historic sites.

▷ Make maps of interesting walking tours around your area.

▷ See if local businesses, libraries, and community centers will make copies of your maps and distribute them.

■ Interview experts to determine the direction of urban development in your area. Is a new shopping mall being planned? A high-rise apartment building? New roads?

▷ Organize a campaign to support or oppose the new development, depending on whether you think it will help or harm your community.

■ Write a proposal for a class on community development to be taught at your school (see page 157).

▷ Present your proposal to the school administration.

▷ Perhaps students could help to teach the class.

▷ Invite experts to speak to your class.

■ Design and paint a mural for an outside wall of your school.

■ Organize a community chorus, orchestra, or band.

■ Work with city or school officials to create a support group and counseling service for families in need.

▷ Start a counseling service for children.

■ Volunteer at your religious organization or community group. Ask what you can do.

Be a Builder

Habitat for Humanity helps to build low-cost housing for people and families who might not otherwise be able to afford their own homes. You might want to join and help build houses in your community or neighboring communities. For more information, write or call:

Habitat for Humanity International
121 Habitat Street
Americus, GA 31709-3498
Telephone: (912) 924-6935

CRIME
FIGHTING

Start a Crime Clue Box

Imagine what might happen if everyone in your school or community looked out for each other. Police have learned that there is less crime in communities where there is an active Neighborhood Watch Program. You can do many safe things to reduce crime, even in your school, such as placing a crime clue box in the school office.

1. You might put a Crime Clue Box in your school office, school library, or classroom.

■ Or start one at your community library, post office, clubhouse, local park building, or community center.

2. On or near the Crime Clue Box, post a sign about how the box should be used.

■ Your sign might say something like this: "The Crime Clue Box is for reporting crimes or other suspicious activities that you witness personally. Your clue will be taken seriously. Please do not misuse the Crime Clue Box."

3.   Create a Crime Clue Report form like the one shown on page 28. Make copies and place them beside your Crime Clue Box.

4.   Notify your local law enforcement agency or crime prevention council about your Crime Clue Box. They can collect the clues on a regular basis and follow up on the information.

5.   If police or private citizens want to offer rewards for clues that lead to arrests, you might post a sign suggesting that witnesses write their birth dates (and/or other identifying number) in the upper right corner of the Crime Clue Report. This can be used to identify the witness who earns a reward.

Crime Clue Report

Today's Date: _____

WHAT happened? _____

_____

WHO did it? _____

Male or female? _____

Age? (Approximate) _____

Hair color and style: _____

Eye color: _____

Race or ethnic group: _____

Describe any scars or marks: _____

_____

What language was the person speaking? _____

Describe the person's clothing, hat, shoes, glasses, etc.: _____

_____

WHERE did it happen? (If you don't know the address, describe houses, stores, and landmarks nearby): _____

_____

WHEN did it happen? _____

Date: _____ Time: _____

If there was a car involved, give as much information as you can:

Color: _____ Make: _____

Year: _____ License plate #: _____

Dents or marks: _____

If the crime involved stolen goods, what was stolen? _____

_____

Do you know where the stolen goods are? _____

Is there anything else you remember? _____

_____

More Ideas for Fighting Crime

■ Survey your school, club, or neighborhood to find out what people think are the leading causes of crime (see pages 161–162).

▷ Put your results on a graph and present it to your school, club, police, community agency, and/or state agency.

■ Start a petition for more police protection in a dangerous area of your community (see pages 153–154).

▷ When you have collected many signatures, present the petition to local police and government officials.

■ See if you can get a local business to sponsor free billboard space for you. Fill it with an anti-crime message.

■ Support people who run for public office with strong anti-crime plans.

▷ Campaign for them.

■ Study the death penalty.

▷ Determine how you feel about it.

▷ Write letters to your representatives in Washington, D.C., explaining your views and asking for their support.

■ Gain representation on a community committee which can fight crime.

> ▷ Try the mayor's youth council or school board.

> ▷ Don't forget the police and law enforcement committee.

■ Join a community crime prevention organization such as the McGruff Program or DARE Program.

> ▷ Work with local law enforcement officers.

■ Start a neighborhood watch program or patrol.

> ▷ Encourage your neighbors to get to know one another.

> ▷ Report any suspicious activities to the police.

■ Interview people who have been crime victims.

> ▷ Collect their stories in a book.

> ▷ Make several copies to distribute to schools, libraries, community centers, etc.

■ Work with local government to start a victim's aid support service.

■ Organize a self-defense workshop.

> ▷ Learn ways to protect yourself from becoming a victim of violent crime.

■ Create a "How to Keep from Becoming a Crime Victim" flier (see pages 152–153).

> ▷ Interview police officers for suggestions and tips on what to include.

> ▷ Distribute your flier to schools and other locations in your community.

> ▷ Or create fliers on other crime-stopping topics, such as "How to Protect Your Home from Burglars" and "How to Discourage a Car Thief."

■ Write to local TV and radio stations. Ask them to focus more attention on kids who are doing things right and less attention on kids who are involved in crime.

■ Write to local TV stations (network and cable) expressing your opinions about violence on television.

> ▷ You might include a student petition supporting your views (see pages 153–154).

■ Paint over graffiti.

> ▷ Work with your local police or "graffiti busters" to eliminate graffiti in your community.

> ▷ If there is an area that is a constant target for graffiti, wipe wax over the surface. The next time someone sprays graffiti on it, you can wash it off.

■ Create a billboard or other surface for good graffiti. Allow people to paint sections.

■ Many states have laws that impose stiff penalties for using or dealing drugs in or around schools (usually within 1,000 feet of the school).

> ▷ Have your school and school grounds declared a Drug-Free Zone.

> ▷ Work with the police to post Drug-Free Zone signs.

■ Learn the facts about drugs, alcohol, and gang involvement.

> ▷ Give speeches to younger students on the dangers of abusing drugs and alcohol and joining destructive gangs.

■ Plan a drug-free club for your school or community.

> ▷ If you start it in your school, every student could sign a banner to hang in the hallway.

■ Create a public service announcement (PSA) for TV or radio against drug and alcohol abuse (see pages 158–159).

■ Survey local stores to find out how much shoplifting they have (see pages 161–162).

> ▷ Write a letter to the editor of your school or local paper describing your suggestions for discouraging shoplifting.

■ Invite police into the schools to tutor students and to present positive role models.

■ Invite police to present a gang awareness assembly to encourage kids to stay out of destructive gangs.

■ Organize a PTA/student program to meet after school and brainstorm ideas and strategies for fighting crime.

■ Create a workshop on fighting crime and invite other schools and groups to attend.

■ Produce an anti-crime, anti-drug, anti-violence play.

    ▷ Perform it for other groups and schools.

■ Work with school administrators to form a conflict management team at your school.

    ▷ Train students to be conflict managers and work with other students to prevent and eliminate arguments and fights.

■ Create and distribute a list of hotlines for kids who might need help. Survey your community to see what's available. Your list might include hotlines for:

    ▷ child abuse

    ▷ child protection services

    ▷ teen pregnancy prevention

    ▷ teen suicide prevention

    ▷ poison control

    ▷ AIDS awareness

    ▷ runaways

    ▷ drug and alcohol abuse

    ▷ rape

    ▷ violence

    ▷ health issues

    ▷ ambulance services

    ▷ crimestoppers

▷ police

▷ fire/arson

▷ energy/utilities

▷ food pantries/food shelves

▷ shelters

▷ legal advice.

■ Create a hotline which gives out hotline numbers for kids who need help. Trained teens could operate the hotline.

■ If your community doesn't offer a hotline for a problem you think is important, start one. Find a community agency that will accept the calls, then advertise the number in your community.

A Hot Tip

Find out more about crime and crime prevention. Write or call:

National Crime Prevention Council
1700 K Street, NW
Second Floor
Washington, DC 20006
(202) 466-6272

Support an Anti-Crime Law

Did you know that kids can help to pass laws? It happens. Fifth grade students at Jackson Elementary in Salt Lake City, Utah, helped push through three laws which made stiffer penalties for drive-by shootings, possession of weapons near schools, and graffiti. They also pushed through an anti-child-abuse law. Their ideas and stories impressed Utah lawmakers more than any adults could have.

■ Choose a specific anti-crime law that you want to work on (see pages 166–167). Some examples:

  ▷ witness protection laws for abused kids

  ▷ gun control

  ▷ laws controlling the use of knives or other weapons

  ▷ the creation of special facilities for kids who have committed crimes.

■ Your law might suggest stiffer penalties for such crimes as:

  ▷ graffiti

  ▷ drive-by shootings

  ▷ possession of weapons near schools

  ▷ drug or alcohol offenses

▷ violence

▷ child abuse

▷ kidnapping

▷ shoplifting

▷ driving without a license

▷ stealing cars

▷ hit-and-run crimes

▷ driving while intoxicated

▷ breaking parole

▷ littering

▷ polluting natural resources

▷ break-ins.

Important

Be aware that a new law might limit your personal freedoms. Study crime-fighting bills or measures very carefully. Listen to all sides of the issues involved before you decide what to do.

More Ideas for Taking Legal Action

■ Join with your student government to make a better discipline policy at your school.

■ Work with your school board to make a better discipline policy for your district.

■ Support a national crime-prevention law (see pages 166–167). Contact a state representative or senator for details.

■ Initiate a local ordinance or law (see pages 163–164.)

▷ For example, you might think it's a good idea to change or create a curfew time for kids to be inside their homes on week nights or weekend nights.

▷ Brainstorm a list of other ideas for making your community a safer place. Would any of these make good ordinances or laws?

■ Study prison conditions. Does your county or state need a new prison reform law?

■ Study immigration laws and conditions. Can you see the need for any reforms?

■ Research violence in the media (TV, radio, magazines, videos, etc.). How does it affect people?

    ▷ Contact your representatives in Congress and ask them to support your views.

    ▷ Find out if legislation related to media violence is already in progress. Ask your representatives to support or oppose the measures.

THE
ENVIRONMENT

Improve Your School's Environment

What is the indoor air like in your school? Have you tested it? Do you need trees around your school or a recycling program in your lunchroom? Take a walk through your halls to see what you might find. See what you can do to improve your school's environment.

- Clean up litter inside and outside your school.
- Erase graffiti and pencil marks from the school bathrooms.
  - ▷ Erase them from the hallways, walls, and anywhere else you find them.
- Plant a garden on the school grounds.
  - ▷ Plant trees at your school.
- Conduct an energy audit of your school.
- Monitor the indoor air.
- Organize an asbestos check. Have professionals do the clean-up.

■ Test the drinking water for lead.

    ▷ Your local health officials can show you how to do this.

■ Bury items (shoes, fruit, paper, tissue, plastic) to see how long it takes them to decompose. Remember that moisture, sunlight, and air will affect your results. What conclusions can you draw?

■ Encourage your school to recycle paper, plastics, cans, chemistry lab wastes, etc.

    ▷ Research the best ways to recycle.

    ▷ Present your findings to the school administration.

■ See if you can get your school to stop using plastics, styrofoam, and other environmentally unfriendly packaging in the school lunchroom.

■ Survey students, parents, and/or staff to get their opinions on any of the above issues (see pages 161–162).

    ▷ Based on the results of your survey, create a proposal for a specific action and present it to the faculty (see page 157).

■ Survey students to see if they would be willing to walk, bike, or ride public transportation to school instead of being driven in cars (see pages 161–162).

■ Hold an environmental fair at your school.

■ Pass a petition to clean up a nearby hazardous waste site (see pages 153–154).

    ▷ Present your petition to your mayor or city officials.

■ Write a proclamation for an environmentally safer and healthier school (see pages 155–156).

    ▷ Present your proclamation to your principal, PTA, and student body.

    ▷ Frame it and hang it in a prominent place in your school.

■ When you shop for school supplies, buy folders and notebooks made from recycled paper.

- See if your school will agree to switch to recycled paper products for the whole school (photocopying paper, stationery, toilet paper, paper towels, etc.).
  - ▷ Research possible sources of recycled paper products.
  - ▷ Present your findings to the school administration. If the recycled paper products are cost-effective, maybe they will agree to switch.
- Teach students at other schools about environmental issues.

Plant Trees

Do you know that one tree in its average 50-year lifetime can clean up $62,000 of air pollution? Trees and people keep each other alive. While trees give off oxygen for you to breathe, you exhale carbon dioxide, which trees thrive upon. Trees do other wonderful things, too; they recycle water, prevent soil erosion, and provide homes for animals and birds. Have you hugged a tree lately? Are there enough trees in your community to hug?

1. Research which trees grow best in your area and what they need to grow.

- You might start by contacting your state or city forester. Ask for advice in choosing which trees to plant, where to plant them, and how to plant them.

■ The forester might also supply you with shovels, fertilizer, and other supplies and materials.

2. Decide which trees you want to plant and where you want to plant them.

■ Make sure there is adequate irrigation in the area.

3. Get permission from local or school officials to plant your trees, if you want to plant them on public ground.

4. Fundraise for money to buy your trees (see pages 167–169).

■ Raise seedlings to transplant.

5. Be sure to call local utility companies (telephone, gas, electricity, cable, sewer) ahead of time to find out if you can plant your trees where you want to.

■ Have them stake out safe areas. You don't want to hit any hidden cables or pipes as you dig.

6. See if a local utility company, nursery, or tree farm will donate the use of an auger—a machine that can dig holes quickly and easily—and someone to operate it for you.

7. Choose a person or group to take care of the trees after they are planted.

■ You might be able to get your town or city to assign maintenance crews to care for the trees.

A Statewide Tree Fund

Planting trees makes a big difference in your community, but there are only so many you can plant by yourself. Students at Jackson Elementary in Salt Lake City, Utah, worked to set up a statewide tree fund. They lobbied lawmakers to set aside $10,000 each year for tree-planting grants and called it the "Leaf It to Us" fund. Over $100,000 worth of trees have been planted in Utah by students in grades K–12. To find out how to start a statewide fund, see pages 165–166.

More Ideas for Planting

- Plant bushes, flower gardens, and/or vegetables instead of trees.

- Replace trees that have died.

- Adopt an acre of rainforest.

- Plant trees in your own yard.

- Do you have a neighbor who is elderly, sick, or injured and has a garden to care for? Volunteer to help.

- Plant a commemorative tree to honor someone.

- Create a children's nature garden.
    - ▷ Label plants and trees.
    - ▷ Schedule guided tours.

Places to Contact

There are many places you can contact for help with your planting projects. Here are a few suggestions.

America the Beautiful Fund
219 Shoreham Building
Washington, DC 20005
(202) 638-1649

A national recognition program for planting projects. Gives away free seed packets. Send a self-addressed, stamped envelope for a faster reply.

National Arbor Day Foundation
100 Arbor Avenue
Nebraska City, NE 68410
(402) 474-5655

Sends out free seedlings to those who join their organization.

Rainforest Alliance
65 Bleecker Street
New York, NY 10012
(212) 677-1900

Information on saving rainforests.

More Ideas for Improving the Environment

■ Set up a statewide neighborhood improvement fund (see pages 165–166). You might choose one or more of these reasons for starting your fund:

▷ repairing sidewalks

▷ adding crosswalks or streetlights

▷ building overstreet walkways to schools

▷ cleaning up vacant lots

▷ cleaning up litter

▷ improving stream beds

▷ repairing homes or abandoned buildings

▷ adding playground equipment to parks

▷ adding drinking fountains or restrooms to parks

▷ adopting (repairing) potholes in streets

▷ painting over graffiti

▷ creating after-school recreational and learning programs for children—art, music, games, drama, etc.

■ Recycle in your home.

■ Use environmentally safe products.

■ Take household toxic waste to a proper facility.

■ Start a compost pile with natural refuse.

■ Encourage your family to use organic fertilizers, if appropriate.

■ Check indoor radon levels.

■ Check your tap water at home for lead or chemicals.

■ Collect rainwater and check for acid rain.

■ Write a story, poem, or play about an environmental issue, or draw pictures.

▷ Share your work with a larger audience.

■ Make presentations on environmental issues to community groups, local garden clubs, the health department, PTA, mayor's council, and other organizations in your area.

■ Create a public service announcement (PSA) for radio or TV on an environmental issue (see pages 158–159).

■ Conduct a community awareness campaign on an environmental issue.

■ Organize a car-pooling campaign to cut down on air pollution.

▷ Organize a "Bike It" campaign.

■ Adopt highways and clean up clutter.

■ Organize a campaign to start a recycling center in your neighborhood or community.

■ Investigate what happens to recycled products.

■ Encourage community groups and businesses to use recycled products.

■ Volunteer to help with neighborhood curbside recycling pick-up.

■ Work with your neighborhood or community to clean up abandoned buildings and vacant lots.

■ Research the presence of underground storage tanks in your community.

▷ Find out if any are leaking.

▷ What could you do to help the owners of the tanks repair or remove them?

■ Contact your state legislature or state house to find out what environmental issues are being considered.

▷ Support or oppose an issue of your choice (see pages 166–167).

■ Study the Greenhouse Effect.

▷ Contact health officials to determine what you can do to help.

■ Study population growth.

▷ Decide how you feel about it, then express your views in letters to editors and officials.

▷ Give speeches to interested groups.

■ Research global resources.

▷ Decide how you feel about the rainforest, water, sustainable agriculture, etc. Write to your representatives in Washington, D.C., or government officials around the world to express your views.

▷ Include a student petition with your letter (see pages 153–154).

Find Out More

There are hundreds of environmental organizations across the country which give out educational materials. For example, you can get information and resources from:

U.S. Environmental Protection Agency
Office of Environmental Education
Coordinator of Youth Programs (1707)
401 M Street, SW
Washington, DC 20460
(202) 260-8749

For educational materials for grades K–12, call:

(202) 260-7751

For grant information, call:

(202) 260-4484

Start an Environmental Club

Have you ever thought of starting your own environmental club? Kids in Petaluma, California, organized a club to save elephants. Maybe you're interested in joining with friends to monitor a stream, promote recycling, or encourage drivers to carpool to school and to work. If you are, here are some ideas to help you.

1. Find friends who are interested in joining your club.

■ Find a sponsor (a teacher, adult leader, parent, etc.).

■ Give your club a name.

■ Pick a time and place to meet.

■ You may want to design a logo, buttons, and T-shirts for your club.

2.   Choose an issue to support, then decide what your club will do about the issue.

■ If you want to monitor a stream, your club might:

   ▷ check the pH level of the water in the stream

   ▷ test for contaminants (work with health officials)

   ▷ identify the fish, protozoa, bacteria, etc. that live in the stream and try to find out if their numbers are increasing or decreasing (and why)

   ▷ remove debris from the stream

   ▷ determine what else needs to be done to improve or protect the stream

   ▷ report your findings to health officials or others who can act on your suggestions.

■ If you want to organize a coalition to clean up a hazardous waste site, your club might:

   ▷ survey people who live near the site to find out what they think (see pages 161–162)

   ▷ pass a petition asking for the clean-up of the site (see pages 153–154)

   ▷ meet with everyone involved (residents, the owners of the site, local officials, etc.) to determine the best solution to the problem

   ▷ write a proposal to public officials who can act on your suggestions (see page 157)

   ▷ go through your local government (if your plan requires local action)

   ▷ go through your state legislature or state house (if your plan requires state action).

■ If you want to work for a statewide environmental license plate or decal, your club might:

   ▷ meet with your state tax commission, health officials, government officials, etc. to find out what your project might involve (see pages 163–164)

▷ suggest that people renewing their license plates be allowed to check a box to make a donation for environmental projects

▷ find a sponsor at your state legislature and lobby for your license plate or decal (see pages 164–165)

▷ build a broad coalition of support for your effort by enlisting students, parents, community members, other schools, and public officials

▷ pass a petition for your license plate or decal (see pages 153–154) and present it to state government officials.

Incorporating Your Club

If you plan to raise money for club activities and causes, you may want to incorporate and gain *tax-exempt status* (so you won't have to pay taxes on money your club receives). Here's how:

1. Get a business license with your city or county.

2. Contact the Internal Revenue Service (IRS) to request guidelines for becoming a nonprofit organization and to obtain a federal identification number.

3. If you want to be classified as a tax-exempt organization, you will need to make a special request to the IRS. Check your *State Code* for details on becoming a tax-exempt organization. Find a copy of your *State Code* at larger libraries in your area (for example, a main county library).

Hold a Recycling Contest

Who in your school, neighborhood, or community can collect the most cans for recycling? Hold a contest to find out. You can also hold contests to collect paper, bottles, glass, plastic, and other recyclables.

1. Give your contest a catchy title.

■ Example: "Tin Can Alley."

■ For other kinds of recycling contests, you might choose a title like "The Greatest Paper Chase" for paper, "Bottle Up" for glass and bottles, or "Great Balls of Foil" for aluminum foil. (Reynolds Aluminum has made this concept famous in many cities. Contact the company for details of their annual contest. You'll find a local number in your phone book.)

2. Decide when your contest will begin and end.

3. Find a sponsor at a recycling center who is willing to support your contest and to allow people to bring cans in to be weighed and stored.

4. Schedule a special event to start your contest.

■ Contact the media (newspapers, radio, TV) and ask them to cover your contest and the opening event.

5. Make your contest appealing by giving prizes and awards.

■ Ask businesses in your community for donations.

■ Or arrange a "challenge" with your school principal. Decide on a goal—a certain number of cans everyone should try to collect. For anyone who exceeds that goal, the principal might agree to:
  ▷ eat lunch with the person
  ▷ wear unmatched shoes for a day
  ▷ dance or sing a song in an assembly
  ▷ allow the person to be acting principal for a day
  ▷ or another idea...consult the principal first!

6. Choose judges for your contest.

■ Invite community leaders to be the judges. This will help to attract attention from the media.

7. Combine your collection contest with an invention contest.

■ For example, who can make the best, most interesting and creative invention out of recycled cans?

Support a Curbside Pick-Up Ordinance

Does your community encourage people to recycle? Does it have a curbside pick-up program? In many communities today, if you put your recyclables out by the curb on a certain day of the week or month, they will be picked up and taken to recycling centers. Some communities even give citizens a discount on their trash collection bill if they participate in curbside pick-up. If your community doesn't provide curbside pick-up, here's what you can do.

1.   Initiate an ordinance with your local government for curbside pick-up of cans, newspapers, paper, plastic, glass, etc. (see pages 163–164).

2.   Contact a person or group in your local government who can help you with your ordinance—the mayor, commission, staff person, council, administrator.

3.   Lobby for your cause (see pages 164–165).

4.   Your ordinance will go through several steps on the way to passing (or not passing). Be sure to appear at the public hearing so you can testify in favor of your ordinance.

More Ideas for Recycling

■ Try to get a state law or city ordinance passed requiring deposits on recyclables (see pages 163–164 and pages 166–167).

■ Start a recycling center at your school.

▷ Contact the city government for a bin.

■ Conduct a survey to find out how people feel about disposable diapers vs. cloth diapers and their effects on the environment (see pages 161–162).

▷ Present your survey to local or state environmental or health officials.

■ Conduct a community information campaign about recycling.

▷ Make fliers to hand out to parents, community members, and other schools.

■ Use your school's closed-circuit TV to tell other students about recycling.

■ Create a public service announcement (PSA) for radio or TV about recycling (see pages 158–159).

■ Host a recycling fair.

    ▷ Invite other schools to participate.

■ Hold a contest for the best recycling jingles.

■ Hold an invention contest with entries made out of recycled goods.

FRIENDSHIP

Promote Tolerance and Understanding

You probably like most of the people you know well. Maybe the people you don't like are simply people you might not understand. Getting to know a person often means getting to like him or her. People who are different from you often have the most to offer you. They might introduce you to new ideas, new activities, new understandings, and new friends.

■ Hold a contest for a school or community mural on the acceptance and appreciation of differences. These might include ethnic differences, religious differences, age differences, racial differences, and any other differences your school or community wants to feature.

■ Make posters, collages, etc. that promote tolerance and understanding of differences.
  ▷ Display them in your school or around your community.

■ Plan Ethnic Awareness days.
  ▷ Identify the different groups within your school or community.

  ▷ Spotlight each group on its special day.

  ▷ You might have special presentations, foods, readings, plays, etc.

■ Start a club to promote tolerance and understanding.

  ▷ Study the clubs that are already active in your school and community. Do they promote tolerance and understanding? Do they accept and appreciate differences? How can you tell? If they don't, what can you do?

■ Make public service announcements over your school communication system on the importance of tolerance and understanding (see pages 158–159). Ask a local radio or TV station to air your PSA's.

■ Show films at your school or community center that promote tolerance and understanding.

  ▷ Show them at home on your VCR and invite friends and neighbors to watch them with you.

  ▷ Afterward, talk about the films and what you learned from them.

■ Make a list of bias-free words and phrases—those that show respect for all kinds of people. Examples: "police officer" instead of "policeman," "hearing impaired" instead of "deaf," "people with disabilities" instead of "handicapped people," "seniors" instead of "old people," etc.

  ▷ Make copies of your list to hand out at your school or club.

■ Give awards for the friendliest people in your school.

  ▷ Come up with a definition of "friendliest" that includes tolerance and understanding.

■ Once a week or once a month, have a "Get Acquainted" lunch period at your school.

  ▷ Have students sit in assigned seats that encourage them to meet and talk to a variety of people.

■ Hold a contest for the best ideas for promoting tolerance and understanding in your school, neighborhood, or community.

▷ Put the ideas into action.

■ Learn about different ethnic holidays.

▷ If possible, study them and celebrate them in your school.

▷ If this is not allowed, celebrate them in your community.

▷ Find out about ethnic festivals in your community. Many are open to interested visitors. Go to one and report back to your class or club.

■ Hold an International Fair at your school. Feature exhibits, presentations, and information about many different cultures and countries.

■ Feature notable people from many different groups and backgrounds on a school or community bulletin board.

■ Invite notable people from many different groups and backgrounds to speak to your school, club, or community.

■ Write ethnic histories.

▷ Present your written histories to local ethnic clubs, groups, and libraries for others to read.

■ Create a school or community forum where people can gather to explore and discuss their similarities and differences.

■ Find out how many different languages are spoken at your school.

▷ Arrange to have important school documents (student handbook, school rules, policies, etc.) translated into the various languages.

■ Volunteer to tutor a student, neighbor, or community member who needs help learning English.

▷ Ask to learn some words and phrases from his or her language.

■ Fundraise to obtain books for your school or community library that promote tolerance, understanding, acceptance, and appreciation of differences (see pages 167–169).

Reach Out

Kids Meeting Kids is an organization of young people from around the world which promotes peace, fair treatment of young people, and a better world. For more information, send a self-addressed, stamped envelope or call:

Kids Meeting Kids
324 West 96th Street
New York, NY 10025
(212) 663-6368

Make New Kid Survival Kits

Have you ever been the "new kid on the block" or the "new kid in school"? Do you remember how it felt when you had no one to show you around, walk with, or simply smile at you? One of the nicest things you can do is to make new students feel as if they're part of your school from the very first day.

1.   Decide what your New Kid Survival Kit will include. Here are some suggestions:

- a map of the school

- information about the school (a description, a brief history, things that make your school special and unique)

- a school telephone directory

- a school calendar

- a student handbook or lists of school rules and requirements

- information about teachers (names, classes they teach, room numbers)

- information about the office staff (names, descriptions of what they do)

■ a list of sports offered at your school

■ a list of activities and clubs offered at your school

■ descriptions of upcoming school events, including dates and times

■ the location of the lost & found

■ PTA (Parent–Teacher Association) information for parents

■ a map of your town or city

■ names and telephone numbers of local medical facilities

■ coupons for treats at local stores and businesses

■ jokes and cartoons

■ information about public transportation (buses, subways, streetcars, etc.)

■ a candy bar or treat

■ anything else you can think of that a new student might want or need.

2.   **Decide how you will greet new students and give them their kits. Ideas:**

■ greet them in person and hand them the kits

■ mail the kits or bring them to their houses

■ sing a crazy song while you hand them their kits

■ hold a special meeting or get-acquainted party for new students.

3.   **Set up a referral system with your school office so you will know immediately when new students arrive. Maybe the school secretary could put information about incoming students in a special box in the school office.**

More Ideas for Welcoming New Students

- Assign "first friends" for new students—someone to eat lunch with them, introduce them to others, and help them get through the first day.

- Start a New Buddy Club for new students.

- Hold a special Newcomers' Day at your school.

- Start an Outreachers' Club to make new students feel welcome and reach out to all students who need a friend or extra help getting along at school.

- Write a proposal for a "Secret Friend Day" at school (see page 157). Present your proposal to the faculty and/or school administration.

Adopt a Grandfriend

Seniors are not only grandparents. They also make grand friends. They are seldom jealous of you, will usually give you honest advice, and will often listen to you more readily than your peers. You could adopt "grandfriends" and find that they become some of your best friends.

■ Find a retirement center, nursing home, seniors' apartment building, or other facility where seniors are interested in forming friendships with young people.

▷ Check with the administrator about visiting hours and any special rules or requirements.

■ Schedule special events to share with your grandfriends.

▷ Hold an afternoon dance. Teach your grandfriends your dances, and ask them to teach you their dances.

▷ Contact the media (newspapers, radio, TV) in advance and tell them about the dance. They might decide to cover it.

■ If possible, take your grandfriends on outings to the zoo, art museums, plays, and other activities.

▷ You can suggest things to do together, but be sure to also ask them what *they* want to do.

- Perform for your grandfriends.
    - ▷ Invite them to your school play or talent show.
    - ▷ Bring your play or talent show to them.

- Take your grandfriends on walks.
    - ▷ Volunteer to push their wheelchairs.

- Write letters to your grandfriends.
    - ▷ Tell them about your life.
    - ▷ Share your thoughts with them.
    - ▷ Enclose jokes, cartoons, riddles, and puzzles.

- Learn as much as you can about your grandfriends.
    - ▷ Hold a "This Is Your Life" party to honor them.
    - ▷ Invite their friends and your friends.

- Play board games and card games with your grandfriends.

- If possible, take your grandfriends to lunch at home or school.

- If many students at your school have grandfriends, host a Grandfriends' Day.
    - ▷ Find out if any of the grandfriends attended your school when they were students. If so, try to find out something about their school days.
    - ▷ Make a display featuring articles, pictures, posters, awards, and anything else you find that date from their time at school.

- Do chores and run errands for your grandfriends.

- Make small repairs, clean, and/or offer to paint for your grand-friends.
    - ▷ Help them out in whatever ways you can.

HEALTH

Promote Healthy Habits

Do you get upset about kids who don't get measles shots, or people who know nothing about the dangers of AIDS, or unhealthy friends who eat a regular diet of candy bars and potato chips? Are you one of those people yourself? Fortunately, good health can be contagious. If you learn about nutrition and disease prevention, your friends might catch on, too.

- Keep yourself physically fit and mentally healthy. Be an inspiration for others.

- Learn about nutrition.
  - ▷ Share what you learn with your family and friends.
  - ▷ Make any needed changes in your own lifestyle and eating habits. Set a good example.

- Start a nutrition club.
  - ▷ Design healthy and tasty menus.
  - ▷ Plan meals to prepare and share. Invite friends to attend.

- Work to improve your school lunchroom menu.
  - ▷ Study the menus. Check the nutritional content of many different items.

> Make a proposal to your faculty or district administration for more nutritious meals (see page 157). Include lunchroom personnel in your planning.

> Are there district policies which determine the selections available in your lunchroom? Find out what the policies are. Work to improve them.

> Survey students to see what they want to eat (see pages 161–162).

■ Teach seniors about good nutrition.

> Make healthful snacks for your senior friends and deliver them personally.

■ Teach a class on the importance of getting healthy and staying healthy.

> Offer it to your neighbors, a community group, or a club.

> Teach it at your school.

■ Distribute information about the importance of regular physical and dental check-ups.

> See if your local health department has free fliers on this topic. Bring the fliers to school, take them around your neighborhood, or hand them out in your community.

■ Start an exercise club.

> Meet once a week (or more often) to swim, do aerobics, hike, or bike.

■ Get fit while fundraising for your favorite charity.

> Have a walk-a-thon or marathon run.

■ Volunteer to teach classes on a sport you enjoy and know a lot about—swimming, jogging, dance, gymnastics, tennis, cross-country skiing, etc.

> Teach at your school, neighborhood park, or community center.

■ Work with your local health department to help immunize children against childhood diseases.

▷ Survey your community to find out which children have not been immunized (see pages 161–162).

▷ Inform parents of times and places where their children can be immunized.

▷ Organize a pick-up and delivery service for families who need transportation.

■ Learn about eating disorders.

▷ Make a flier or give speeches to warn others about the dangers of eating disorders.

■ If you have a friend you think might have an eating disorder or who seems to be in danger of some other nutritional deficiency or disease, express your concern to him or her. See if your friend is willing to get help.

▷ Tell an adult you trust about your friend. Eating disorders can be life-threatening. Ask the adult to help you help your friend.

■ Learn about diseases such as AIDS, hepatitis, alcoholism, and tuberculosis and how they can be prevented.

▷ Make a chart or flier and share your findings with others.

▷ Make speeches about what you have learned.

▷ Write letters to patients at hospitals who have these diseases. Visit them and cheer them up.

■ Start an anti-smoking campaign.

▷ Collect "I Won't Smoke" pledges from friends, neighbors, and community residents.

▷ Have nonsmokers sign a large wall poster to display in your school or community center.

▷ Create an anti-smoking jingle or a public service announcement (PSA) on the dangers of smoking (see pages 158–159).

▷ Work for smoke-free areas in public buildings, restaurants, and recreational areas—or work to make them completely smoke-free. Interview people for opinions.

▷ Write a play against smoking. Present it to schools and clubs in your community.

▷ Create an anti-smoking flier to distribute to schools and clubs (see pages 152–153).

▷ Work with your legislators to investigate the possibility of having cigarettes placed behind counters or in locked cases in stores.

▷ Contact the media and ask them to cover your campaign.

■ Start a campaign against drug and alcohol abuse.

▷ Collect pledges.

▷ Contact police to start a DARE (Drug Abuse Resistance Education) program in your area.

▷ Create a public service announcement (PSA) on the dangers of drugs and alcohol (see pages 158–159).

▷ Write a play against drug and alcohol abuse. Present it to schools and clubs in your community.

▷ Create an anti-drugs-and-alcohol flier to distribute to schools and clubs (see pages 152–153).

▷ Work with city or state officials to start a hotline kids can call for help. Or create a hotline at your school.

▷ Make a flier listing the support services available in your community for people who abuse alcohol and other drugs (see pages 152–153). Distribute it at your school, around your neighborhood, and in your community.

▷ Organize a club for people who are recovering from drug or alcohol addiction.

▷ Contact the media and ask them to cover your campaign.

■ Start a campaign against early sexual activity.

▷ Invite health officials, youth leaders, and educators to speak to your neighborhood, school, club, or religious organization about early sexual activity and related issues (teen pregnancy, sexually transmitted diseases, etc.).

▷ Create a public service announcement (PSA) on the dangers of early sexual activity (see pages 158–159).

▷ Write a play against early sexual activity. Present it to schools and clubs in your community.

▷ Create a flier on the dangers of early sexual activity to distribute to schools and clubs (see pages 152–153).

■ Write a pamphlet or start a support service for people who are dealing with death, sickness, emotional stress, teen suicide, or other issues of physical or mental health.

More Ideas for Promoting Good Health

■ Be a Red Cross volunteer.

▷ Contact your local Red Cross. Ask how you can help.

▷ You might volunteer your services for a blood drive.

■ Learn about the nutritional needs of animals kept as pets—cats, dogs, birds.

▷ Create fliers to distribute to pet owners (see pages 152–153).

■ Learn about chemicals, preservatives, sprays, and other synthetic and organic treatments used on foods.

▷ Decide if you are for or against them.

▷ Share your information with others and organize a group of supporters.

▷ Present your findings to city or state health agencies.

■ Learn about organ transplants.

▷ Start and run an information campaign to educate other people about the need for organ donors.

▷ Encourage people to sign Organ Donor cards.

■ Research abortion and the abortion controversy.

▷ Determine how you feel about abortion.

▷ Write letters to the media expressing your views.

■ Research genetic engineering.

▷ Determine how you feel about genetic engineering. Do you think it should be used to prevent diseases? To produce superior people? To improve agriculture?

▷ Debate the issues in class.

▷ Write letters to your representatives in Congress, your state house, or to medical officials stating your conclusions. You might include a student petition (see pages 153–154).

Find Out More

Learn more about promoting good health and healthy habits by contacting one or both of these organizations:

National Self-Help Clearinghouse
25 West 43rd Street, Room 620
New York, NY 10036
(212) 354-8525 or
(212) 642-2944

Provides information about and referrals to self-help groups around the country. Ask for tips on how to organize your own self-help groups.

Public Health Service
Public Affairs
Hubert H. Humphrey Building
200 Independence Avenue, SW
Room 701-H
Washington, DC 20201
(202) 690-6867

Provides information on health issues.

HOLIDAYS

Make Gift Baskets for Seniors

Holidays can be lonely times for an older person whose family might be miles away or gone. They can be good times to share a little cheer with the senior citizens you know. When you do, you might find that you're less lonely, too.

1.   Choose a nursing home, center, or shelter for senior citizens.

- Telephone and ask permission to make gift baskets.

- Ask if the seniors have any special needs.

- Find out about visiting hours.

2.   Decide what you will put in your gift baskets. Check with the administrator to find out if it's okay to include:

- personal items (combs, brushes, toothpaste, shampoo, deodorant, mirrors, etc.)

- food (fruit, candy, breads, baked goods—be sure to ask about special diets)

- clothing

- bedding

- flowers (ask about allergies)

- letters and cards written by you and your friends

- books (paperbacks, large-print books, books on tape).

3.   Decide what you will use for "baskets." Ideas:

- real baskets

- boxes

- cloth sacks

- paper sacks.

4.   Arrange a time to deliver your baskets.

- Who will drive?

- How long will you stay?

Trim a Mitten Tree

If you're looking for a rewarding holiday experience, you might find a group of disadvantaged children and take up a collection for them. If you investigate this issue, you'll discover that there are many children right in your community who play in the cold or snow with bare hands. Children always need mittens, and if you collect some to give away, you'll probably find that you warm up more than their hands.

1.   Locate an organization that serves disadvantaged children and their families. Telephone and ask permission to make a mitten tree.

2.   Decide how you will get the mittens for the tree. Some possible ways:

■ Ask for donations—from students, local businesses, community organizations.

■ Make the mittens yourself.

■ Raise money to buy mittens (see pages 167–169).

3. See if there is a tree available for you to use.

■ Ask a tree seller to donate a tree.

4. Find a way to deliver your tree to the organization.

More Ideas for Helping Children

You can adapt these ideas to include anyone who is lonely on a holiday.

■ Trim a sock tree, a shoe tree, a scarf tree, or a personal items tree (soap, shampoo, toothpaste, etc.).

▷ What other tree ideas can you come up with?

■ Work with disadvantaged children to trim a tree, then choose someone to deliver it to.

■ Help disadvantaged children make gifts to give to other people.

- Collect shoes, eyeglasses, etc. for children in a third world country. Ask legislative officials to research where and how to send the items you have collected.

- Donate your time.
  ▷ Read to disadvantaged children during the holidays or any time of the year.
  ▷ Sing to them.
  ▷ Present plays to them. Help them put on plays of their own.
  ▷ Write down stories they dictate to you.
  ▷ Take them on outings—to the zoo, the park, to see Santa. You'll need adult chaperones and permissions.

- Visit children in hospitals.
  ▷ Make holiday cards for them.
  ▷ Volunteer to help them make gifts and do crafts.

More Ideas for Holiday Cheer

Write or call:

Corporation for National Service
1100 Vermont Avenue, NW
Eleventh Floor
Washington, DC 20525
(202) 606-5000
Provides information on all kinds of youth service projects, including projects related to the holidays.

HOMELESS
PEOPLE

Make "I Care" Kits

Can you think of many things more frightening than losing your home? It is estimated that 735,000 persons in the United States are homeless on any given night, and more and more of them are children. You can't solve the problem of homelessness, but you can help homeless people to feel a sense of dignity by collecting and distributing personal care kits.

1. Learn about homeless shelters in your community. Contact one or more and ask permission to make "I Care" kits. Visit the shelter to find out what the people there need.

2. Decide what you will put in your "I Care" kits. Ideas:

- combs
- toothbrushes
- dental floss
- soap
- tissues
- petroleum jelly
- nail clippers

- brushes
- toothpaste
- mirrors
- shampoo
- lotion
- deodorant
- nail files

- tweezers
- safety pins
- needles and thread.

3.   Decide what you will use to hold your "I Care" kits. Ideas:

- plastic bags
- cardboard boxes
- cloth bags
- shoe boxes.

4.   Fundraise for money to buy the items for your "I Care" kits, or ask for donations (see pages 167–169).

5.   Arrange a time to deliver the kits. Who will drive?

Who's Homeless?

According to the National Alliance to End Homelessness:

- Today's homeless are younger (60% are under 30 years of age) and are more educated.

- 30% are single parents with children.

- 25% of homeless people are children, and this is the fastest-growing segment of the homeless population.

More Ideas for Helping Homeless People

■ Collect other items to deliver to homeless shelters. Ideas:
  ▷ blankets
  ▷ sheets
  ▷ towels
  ▷ toys
  ▷ books
  ▷ disposable diapers.

■ Hold a clothing drive to collect cold-weather clothing—mittens, boots, gloves, coats, scarves, hats, sweaters.

■ Volunteer to help prepare or serve food at a shelter.

■ Volunteer to help with repairs or maintenance at a shelter.

■ Make a special effort to help the children at the shelter. Ideas:
  ▷ Tutor them or read to them.
  ▷ Take them on outings.
  ▷ Become a Big Buddy for one or more of the children.

■ Contact your local government offices and ask about programs to build low-cost housing in your area.

   ▷ Ask what you can do to help.

   ▷ If there are no programs to build low-cost housing in your area, try to start one.

   ▷ Survey community members to learn their opinions about low-cost housing and the need for a program (see pages 161–162).

   ▷ Start a petition to collect signatures of people who support low-cost housing (see pages 153–154).

   ▷ Make a proposal for a low-cost housing program (see page 157) and submit it to officials.

■ Contact Habitat for Humanity (see page 24) and find out if they are building or planning to build low-cost housing in your area.

   ▷ Volunteer to help.

   ▷ Ask your friends, family members, classmates, and neighbors to volunteer with you.

■ Find out if there are any low-cost housing units which are scheduled for demolition.

   ▷ Support or begin a project to restore them instead.

■ Work for programs that help people who are homeless and out of work. Ideas:

   ▷ child care

   ▷ health care

   ▷ housing

   ▷ counseling.

■ Contact job training and placement centers in your community.

   ▷ Find out about opportunities available to homeless people and others who are out of work.

   ▷ Start an information campaign to make homeless people aware of work opportunities.

■ Help an out-of-work person find a job.

  ▷ Contact job training and placement centers.

  ▷ Check the want ads in your local newspaper.

  ▷ Call state or local employment agencies.

  ▷ Help the person to prepare a résumé.

  ▷ Arrange for day care if the person has children.

  ▷ Arrange for transportation to and from job interviews.

■ Work for more opportunities for job training and placement in your state.

  ▷ Contact your state legislators to find out if any new laws are being considered that would expand job opportunities. If there are, support the laws and work to get them passed.

  ▷ If there aren't any new laws being considered, ask your legislators to initiate one (see pages 163–164).

■ Contact your local government officials and ask about their plans for expanding job training and placement in your community.

  ▷ Find out what you can do to help.

HUNGER

Hold a Food Drive

Almost everyone has an extra can of food on their shelves, and most people don't mind donating a few. There are food banks in many cities which rely on generous folks like you to keep their shelves full. If your community doesn't have a food bank, you might even stir up interest to begin one yourself.

1.   Choose a group, shelter, or organization to receive the food you will collect during your food drive.

■ Ask them if they want the donation.

■ Ask if they have any special requests or requirements. For example, canned goods are easier to store. Packaged goods can get ripped or crushed and attract insects.

2.   Decide who you want to participate in your food drive. Students? Faculty? Neighbors? Stores? Churches? Clubs? All of the above?

3.   Decide when you will have your food drive. During Thanksgiving, Christmas, or some other holiday? When will it begin? When will it end?

■ Will you schedule your food drive to coincide with other special events? For example, if you hold it during the school play, you can suggest that people coming to the play bring a can of food to donate.

4. Decide where you will have your food drive. At your school? Place of worship? Community center? Other possibilities?

5. Decide how you will collect the food. Will you go in private cars and knock on doors? Will you ask people to bring their donations to a central location at your school, community center, etc.?

6. Decide where you will store the food you collect until you are ready to donate it.

7. Make a flier about your food drive (see pages 152–153).

■ Include the name of the organization that will receive the food, the dates of your food drive, locations, collection information, and the name and number of a contact person in case people have any questions.

8. Get some publicity for your food drive.

■ Write a press release and send it to local radio, TV, and cable stations and newspapers (see pages 154–155). The more people know about your food drive, the more donations you'll collect.

More Ideas for Fighting Hunger

- Collect grocery coupons to give to a local food bank.

- Volunteer to help at a food bank.

- If your community doesn't have a food bank, work with local officials to start one.

- Volunteer to help prepare food and serve meals at a shelter.

- Conduct a food drive for a shelter.

- Collect other important items besides food, such as vitamins and money for medicines.

- Prepare sack lunches and deliver them to homeless people or disadvantaged children.

- Contact restaurants or grocery stores to find out how much produce they throw out each day or each week.
    - Ask if they would be willing to donate the produce to a shelter.
    - Organize a pick-up and delivery service for the produce.

Find Out More

To learn about world hunger, contact:

World Hunger Education Service
PO Box 29056
Washington, DC 20017
(202) 298-9503

Start an Anti-Hunger Campaign

Have you ever gone without food for 24 hours? Try it. You might be surprised at how you feel. Collecting food for hungry people is an important way to fight hunger, but if you want to make a more lasting difference, give this plan a try.

1.   Call your local health department and ask for the latest statistics on hunger in your community.

■   The health department might direct you to another organization. Keep calling and following leads until you get some answers.

2.   Survey your school or community to find out what people know about hunger (see pages 161–162). Your survey might include questions like these:

■   How many children in our community do you think go to bed hungry at night? 10%? 20%? 30%? 50%? More?

■ Where are the hungry children? In one or more neighborhoods? Which ones? Or are they in many different neighborhoods?

■ Should taxes be used to reduce or eliminate hunger among children? If so, what kind of taxes? Local? State? Federal?

■ Should grants from foundations be used to reduce or eliminate hunger among children?

3. Pass a petition to reduce or eliminate hunger among children (see pages 153–154). Your petition might include one or more of these ideas:

■ Setting aside a percentage of tax money for this purpose.

■ Having schools provide free breakfasts or lunches to hungry children. (This usually depends on federal funding. Try to find a community group or agency to help you promote this idea.)

4. If you want to work on a local level:

■ Contact your mayor, council, or administrator.

■ Share the information you gathered in your phone call(s) and survey.

■ Present your petition and the signatures you gathered.

■ Ask your mayor, council, or administrator to help hungry children in your community. Offer to help.

5. If you want to work on a statewide level:

■ Find a sponsor in your state legislature.

■ Share the information you gathered in your phone call(s) and survey.

■ Present your petition and the signatures you gathered.

■ Ask your sponsor to initiate a new law or statewide fund to fight hunger among children (see pages 163–164 and 165–166).

6.   Get media attention for your local or statewide anti-hunger campaign.

■ Contact a newspaper. Ask to speak to a reporter who specializes in education, children, or nutrition. Explain what you are doing to fight hunger. For example, you might tell the reporter when and where you will present your survey and petition. (Be sure to call at least two weeks in advance of any event you want the reporter to attend.)

■ Send out a press release (see pages 154–155).

■ Write a public service announcement (PSA) for cable TV or radio (see pages 158–159).

Grow a School Garden

Look around your school yard. Are there places where you could plant some gardens? You could harvest the produce and donate it to hungry people. A school yard is a great place for a garden because everyone in the school—students and staff—can help you to care for it.

1.   Get permission to plant your garden. Check with the principal.

2.   Decide where to put your garden.

3.   Decide what to plant in your garden.

■ Research what different vegetables need in order to grow. Find out about growing seasons, shade vs. sun, how much water they need, whether they require fertilizer, if they must be thinned or weeded, etc.

4.   Decide where to get the materials you need.

■ Will you plant seeds or seedlings (little plants)? Where will you get your seeds or seedlings? Do you need to fundraise for money to buy them (see pages 167–169)? Or can you ask for donations from local nurseries?

■ Where will you get shovels, spades, hoes, gardening gloves, and other tools you need?

5.   Choose a group, shelter, or organization to receive the produce you will grow in your garden.

■ Ask them if they want the donation.

■ Ask if they have any special requests or requirements. For example, would they rather have more carrots than lettuce?

6.   Decide who at your school will help to plant and care for the garden. Students? Faculty? Staff? Everyone?

■ Post a sign-up list. Ask people to sign their names under specific gardening duties: planting, weeding, watering, harvesting, cleanup. (They can sign up for more than one.)

■ Who will take care of the garden over the weekends? During school breaks?

■ Be sure to contact school maintenance or custodial people and tell them about your garden. Otherwise they might mow right over it. If they know about your garden, they will probably help you to protect it.

7.   Plan for what will happen after the harvest.

■ Will the school garden be an ongoing project? If it is a success this year, your school might decide to continue it next year. Who will be in charge of it then?

■ If the school garden is only a one-year project, you will need to return the ground to its original condition or better. For example, if you dug up grass to plant your garden, you will need to reseed or resod.

More Ideas for Giveaway Gardening

■ Work with your club or scout troop to plant gardens on private property or public lands. Get permission first.

■ Plant a garden in your yard and donate the produce.

■ Plant a garden at a homeless shelter and help care for it.

■ Plant a community garden. Invite residents to help care for it and share the harvest.

LITERACY

Try Tutoring

Did you know that 20 percent of the adult population in the United States can't read English well enough to function adequately in our society? No other basic skill is more closely associated with success in life. You might be able to motivate a child to read in a way no one else can.

1. **Find your "target group." Who needs tutoring?**

■ You might find out by surveying your school, neighborhood, or local youth groups (see pages 161–162).

2. **What skill(s) do they need the most help learning?**

■ Besides reading, ask if they need help with math, science, history, or…. (This could be part of your survey.)

3. **If you decide to work with a school or youth group, get permission to tutor.**

■ Check with the principal, teachers, or group leaders.

4. **Recruit tutors.**

■ Ask your friends to volunteer.

■ Ask teachers for recommendations.

■ Identify each tutor's skills so you can match up tutors with students.

5.   Schedule tutoring times and places.

■ Will you want to tutor after school, during free periods or study halls, on the weekends?

■ At school: Ask if you can use a room, a corner of the library, a part of the lunchroom.

■ In your community: See if you can use a room at the local library or community center.

6.   Decide how students will let you know that they want to be tutored.

■ Will you post sign-up sheets in classrooms and on community bulletin boards?

■ Will you prepare sign-up forms to send home with parents?

■ Will you ask teachers for recommendations, especially if the kids are young?

■ Be sure to include information on tutoring times and places and on how long the tutoring will last.

7.   Collect any supplies and materials you will need—books, papers, pencils.

■ Will the students you are tutoring bring their own supplies and materials?

■ Will you need to fundraise for supplies and materials (see pages 167–169)?

8.   How will you reward the students—and the tutors?

■ Plan treats for students who complete the tutoring or show good progress. Fast-food restaurant coupons, movie tickets, and small gift certificates to local stores make good treats. Ask for donations.

■ Honor your tutors with a special assembly or luncheon, certificates, or points toward a prize.

■ Make posters featuring the tutors to display in public places.

More Ideas for Promoting Literacy and Learning

■ Hold a used book sale. Donate the money to a literacy group.

■ Collect used books to give to a hospital, nursing home, shelter, or preschool.

■ Read aloud to a person who is visually impaired. Or read into a tape recorder.

■ Survey your community to learn how many people are illiterate (see pages 161–162). Present your results to your school board, mayor or council, and/or legislator. Ask for action.

■ Organize a reading hour for children at your local school or library. Recruit friends to volunteer as readers.

■ Make simple reading and math flash cards for a preschool or day care center.

■ Teach English, Spanish, or another language you know to a person who needs help learning.

■ Tutor other people in any skill or talent you have—from reading to dancing, playing an instrument or a playing a sport.

Read More About It

For information on literacy, writing, and standards for reading and writing, contact:

> Council for Basic Education
> 1319 F Street, Suite 900
> Washington, DC 20004
> (202) 347-4171

PEOPLE WITH
SPECIAL NEEDS

Hold an Athletics Contest

Have you ever blindfolded yourself and walked around your house? Have you sat in a wheelchair or walked with crutches? Have you turned down the sound on the TV and tried lip-reading the news? Those are a few ways to understand a little about people with special needs. A better way is to spend time getting to know them. When you hold an athletic contest—patterned after the Special Olympics—you will meet many people you might not meet otherwise.

1.   **Decide who will participate in your athletics contest.**

■ If you want to host a certain group, get permission from a facility which serves them (a group home, medical facility, or school). Or ask the parents for permission.

■ Ask about the athletes' needs. Which sports are appropriate? What precautions will you need to take? Use this information to plan your activities and events.

■ If children will be participating in your contest, you will need to get permission from their parents or guardians.

2.   Who will help with your contest? Friends, students, clubs, local service organizations? How will you recruit people to help?

■ Make a flier to hand out (see pages 152–153).

■ Post sign-up sheets at your school, community center, and other public places.

3.   When and where will you hold your contest?

■ How long will your contest last? One afternoon? A whole day? Two days?

■ Will most of the events be indoors, outdoors, or both?

■ Find a location (a park, recreational facility, school) that has the space and facilities you need. If all of your athletes are from the same place, maybe you can hold your contest there.

■ Make a schedule listing the events, times, and locations.

4.   How will you transport the athletes to and from the events? By car? Bus? On foot?

■ You may need to arrange for several drivers.

■ Or see if a local bus company will donate buses and drivers for the occasion.

5.   What equipment will you need for the various events? Ropes, balls, strings, beanbags, etc.?

■ Is the equipment available at the location where you will hold your contest? Are you allowed to use it?

■ Will you need to ask for donations of equipment?

■ Will you need to fundraise for money to purchase equipment (see pages 167–169)?

6. Plan for a day to train the people who will be helping with your contest.

▪ Your helpers will need to know about the athletes' abilities and special needs. You can get this information from their care providers. They might offer to teach the classes for you.

▪ You will need one or two helpers at each event. Make sure you have enough people.

▪ You might also assign one helper to each athlete to lend a hand during the competition.

7. Set the rules for the events.

▪ Will you group the athletes by age, skill level, or activities?

▪ How will you score the events? Who will keep score?

▪ How will you determine the winners? How will you make sure that everyone who participates is a winner?

8. Decide if you will give prizes and have food available for athletes and guests.

▪ Will you need to ask for donations of prizes and food?

▪ Will you need to fundraise for money to purchase prizes and food (see pages 167–169)?

9. Get media attention for your contest.

▪ Send out a press release to newspapers, TV stations, and radio stations (see pages 154–155).

▪ Write a public service announcement (PSA) for cable TV or radio (see pages 158–159).

Special Olympics International

To find out more about how to hold a successful athletics contest for people with special needs, contact the experts. Write or call:

> Special Olympics International
> 1350 New York Avenue, Suite 500, NW
> Washington, DC 20005
> (202) 628-3630

More Ideas for Helping People with Special Needs

- Visit a rehabilitation center. Learn about patients with special needs. Volunteer to help.

- Survey people with special needs who live in your neighborhood or community.
    - ▷ Find out about their special needs.
    - ▷ Lobby local, state, and national government agencies on their behalf (see pages 164–165).

- Work for legislation designed to help people with special needs (see pages 166–167).

- Tour local shopping malls to see if they are accessible to people with special needs.
    - ▷ If they are, contact mall officials to thank them.
    - ▷ If they are not, contact mall officials and ask about plans to make them accessible.

■ Tour your town or city to see if it is generally accessible to people with special needs. What about public buildings? Stores? Restaurants? Parks? Office buildings? Write a letter to the editor of your local newspaper, describing what you found at various locations.

■ Is your school or community center accessible to people with special needs? If not, do something about it.

■ Hold an invention contest. Who can make the best, most creative, and most useful invention for people with special needs?

▷ Invite people with special needs to participate in the contest.

▷ Invite local newspaper reporters to take pictures of the inventions and write a story about your contest.

■ Volunteer to help people with special needs in any way you can.

▷ Read to them.

▷ Shop for them.

▷ Clean or do yard work.

■ Set up a buddy system at your school for kids with special needs.

■ Volunteer at an agency that works with emotionally disturbed children.

■ Fundraise for Braille books for the visually impaired (see pages 167–169).

■ Volunteer to work with children at risk of suicide, alcohol or other drug use, gang involvement, pregnancy, running away, and other problems.

▷ You may want to help out at a hotline.

▷ Volunteer at a community agency or counseling center that specializes in working with children and teens.

■ Contact the National Self-Help Clearinghouse (see page 76) and/or Youth Service America (see page 12) for more information on helping people with special needs.

POLITICS AND GOVERNMENT

Work for Voter Registration

Did you know that only a small percentage of voters turn out to vote in municipal elections, even fewer than in national elections? Although this is one of the main rights the founders of our nation fought for, many adults have become apathetic. They just don't care. You'll be voting soon, and in the meantime you can work to get adults out to support the candidates of their choice.

- Contact your local League of Women Voters or voter registration office. Ask what you can do to help get people registered to vote.

- Telephone residents and explain how to register.

- Work at the polling place during elections.

- Go door-to-door to register residents.
    - ▷ Arrange for an adult chaperon to accompany you.
    - ▷ Borrow a Registration Book to register people on the spot.
    - ▷ Leave Mail-In Registration Forms at people's homes.
    - ▷ Inform residents of registration times and places in their neighborhood.

▷ Hand out absentee ballots for seniors, people with disabilities, or people who will be out of town during the elections.

■ Provide a voter pick-up or transportation service for seniors or other people with special needs who might not be able to travel to the voting booth.

▷ Or you can offer to mail their votes for them.

More Ideas for Taking Political Action

■ Identify a local issue that you care about.

▷ Contact someone in local government (a sponsor).

▷ Initiate a new ordinance, or support or oppose one in the process of becoming a law (see pages 163–164).

■ Identify a statewide issue that you care about.

▷ Contact your area representative, senator, or staff person.

▷ Initiate, support, or oppose a state law (see pages 163–164 and 166–167).

- Identify a national issue that you care about.
  ▷ Contact your national government representatives (senators, members of Congress) and ask them to support or oppose the issue, depending on how you feel about it.

- Campaign for a candidate who is running for office. You might:
  ▷ Telephone residents to encourage them to vote for your candidate.
  ▷ Pass out fliers describing your candidate.
  ▷ Run errands for your candidate or your candidate's staff.
  ▷ Write an article about your candidate for your school or local newspaper.
  ▷ Conduct a letter-writing campaign for your candidate.
  ▷ Call your candidate's office to find out about more ways you can help.

- Support or work to defeat an issue that affects your neighborhood or community. Examples: a proposal for a light-rail system, a new high-rise, or an education bond.
  ▷ Give speeches to local community councils, school boards, and other organizations.
  ▷ Write letters to editors of local newspapers and magazines.

- Pass a student petition to support or oppose an issue (see pages 153–154).
  ▷ Present it to government officials.
  ▷ Write a press release inviting the media to the presentation (see pages 154–155).

- Petition for a student position on the community council, neighborhood committee, school board, or any state or local agency (see pages 153–154).
  ▷ Many communities are now allowing students to become school board members. Check with your local school board. If they don't allow student members, see if they will agree to change their policy.

▷ When and if you get on the board, tackle another big issue: work for a student *vote* on the board in addition to representation.

■ Interview public officials to learn their views on an issue that interests you.

    ▷ Write an article for your school paper about what you learned.

    ▷ Give a speech to your class or PTA.

    ▷ Make a presentation to your community council or club.

■ Organize a public issues forum for speakers.

■ Survey your school or club to find out how people feel about an issue that interests you (see pages 161–162).

    ▷ Present your results to an interested group in your school or community.

■ Design a model government for your class, school, or club.

    ▷ Form your own laws.

    ▷ Write your own constitution,

    ▷ Elect officials.

    ▷ Set up your own court system.

■ Contact your juvenile court system. Find out if they have a "Kids in Court" program to match older kids who have been in court (as abuse victims, or for other reasons) with younger kids who are facing a court experience. The older kids help the younger kids.

    ▷ If your state doesn't have a "Kids in Court" program, see if you can start one (see pages 163–164 and 165–166).

■ Write letters to government officials in your country and other countries asking for the humane treatment of prisoners.

■ Take a tour of your city or state government offices.

    ▷ Learn what happens there. Who works there? What are their duties?

    ▷ Ask if you can help out as a volunteer or an intern.

■ Study U.S. foreign policy.

  ▷ Decide how you feel about dealing with allies, intervention in other countries, foreign aid, and other issues.

  ▷ Write letters to your representatives in Congress expressing your views and asking for their support.

  ▷ Include a student petition stating your ideas (see pages 153–154).

■ Research the mass media (TV, radio, newspapers, magazines, videos, etc.).

  ▷ Determine what you think the role of the media should be.

  ▷ Consider questions like, "Do the media represent all sides of an issue?" "Should the government regulate the media? If so, how? If not, why not?"

  ▷ Write letters to the media expressing your views.

■ Research the ways in which advertising affects people.

  ▷ Consider questions like, "Is advertising ever harmful?" "Is it ever helpful?" "Do people make decisions because of advertising?" "Do most people ignore advertising?"

  ▷ Decide how you feel about advertising.

  ▷ Write to your representatives in Congress to find out if there is any national legislation in progress relating to advertising. Depending on your point of view, ask your representatives to support or oppose the legislation.

■ Research the Bill of Rights.

  ▷ Consider questions like, "Are some people's rights being violated or limited? If so, which ones? Free speech? Freedom of the press? Any others?"

  ▷ Write letters to officials, editors, and public issues forums.

  ▷ Contact the media.

  ▷ Survey the public to gather opinions and ask for support (see pages 161–162).

▷ Start a Bill of Rights Club to learn more about it and work to protect it.

▷ Pass a petition in support of the Bill of Rights (see pages 153–154).

▷ Support or oppose legislation that affects the Bill of Rights (see page 166–167).

Get in Touch

Look in the Yellow Pages of your local phone book or the blue Government pages to find the telephone numbers for your city and state government offices.

Write to your senators and members of Congress in Washington, D.C.:

> The Senate
> The Capitol
> Washington, DC 20510

> The House of Representatives
> The Capitol
> Washington, DC 20515

To reach any member of Congress, call:
> (202) 224-3121

For information on pending legislation, call the Legislative Status Office:
> (202) 225-1772

SAFETY

Promote After-School Safety

Children often get injured or get into trouble if left alone after school, and more and more children are becoming latchkey kids. Can you think of some activities children could do after school while playing it safe?

■ Volunteer to give after-school performing arts lessons in dance, drama, or music.

▷ Make a plan and present it to the parents in your neighborhood or other adults in your community.

▷ Arrange for a safe place to give your lessons. Suggestions: a school or community center.

▷ Hold a talent show so your students can demonstrate what they have learned.

■ Assist an after-school little league or other sports program for younger children.

▷ Volunteer to keep track of gear, telephone players and remind them of practices, organize treats, and/or help with practices.

■ Volunteer at a latchkey program in an elementary school or day-care center.

> ▷ You might help with activities, organize and pass out materials and supplies, or watch the children. Find out what the adult leaders most need you to do.

■ Volunteer at a YMCA, YWCA, Boy or Girl Scouts, Camp Fire, Girls' Club, Boys' Club, or other organization that provides programs and services for children in your community.

■ Is there an unused building in your neighborhood or community? See if you can get permission to hold after-school events there.

> ▷ You'll need to find adult sponsors.

> ▷ Does the building need renovations? Maybe local businesses will offer to help.

> ▷ You'll have to collect equipment, materials, and supplies for your after-school program. Will you ask for donations? Fundraise for money to buy what you need (see pages 167–169)?

> ▷ If you can't find a *whole* unused building, maybe you can find *part* of a building that isn't being used. Start your program there.

■ Hold after-school classes for the children in your neighborhood. Teach them a skill you know. Examples: bike repair; cooking; drawing; cartooning; sewing; skating; simple gymnastics. Emphasize safety.

■ Create a play that teaches young children how to stay safe at home while their parents are away.

■ Make a flier of after-school safety tips for young children (see pages 152–153). Give copies to grade schools and day-care centers. You might include these tips and more that you think of yourself:

> ▷ Know your name, address, and telephone number.

> ▷ Always let your parents know where you are.

> ▷ Don't wear a house key around your neck.

▷ Work out a family escape plan in case of a fire.

▷ Never walk alone.

▷ Never open doors to strangers.

▷ When you are home alone and the telephone rings, never tell a caller that your parents aren't there. Say that they're busy or can't come to the phone.

▷ Know where to go for help if you ever get lost or in trouble.

▷ If you suspect that someone is following you, go to a nearby McGruff House or other safe house.

▷ Don't talk to strangers.

▷ If a stranger follows you, tries to touch you, or tries to get you to go with him or her, run away and scream for help.

▷ Never wear clothing that makes it hard for you to run.

▷ No one has the right to touch you or say things to you that make you feel uncomfortable or afraid. If this ever happens to you, tell a parent or another adult you trust.

▷ Never go into your home if door is standing open or a window is broken.

▷ Be alert. Trust your instincts. If something feels uncomfortable or scary to you, get away as fast as you can.

Promote Safety in Your Community

Accidents are the fourth leading cause of death in the United States today. Accidents shouldn't happen. "Be prepared" is the best rule for handling any accident or emergency. It means that you have to think about things ahead of time and decide what you would do if you didn't have time to think. Are you interested in tornado or fire protection, bike safety, or safe driving? Students in Virginia Beach worked through their legislature to establish a better toy safety law. What are your ideas for making your community a safer place to live?

■ Telephone community agencies to learn the leading causes of accidents in your community.

  ▷ Create a graph illustrating your findings.

  ▷ Make copies and distribute them to schools, clubs, and religious organizations.

■ Survey your school, neighborhood, club, or community to learn about the most common accidents in homes (see pages 161–162).

▷ Make a flier on how to avoid the most common accidents (see pages 152–153). Distribute it in your school and neighborhood.

■ Survey your community to find out the leading causes of toy-related injuries (see pages 161–162).

▷ If your survey shows that a particular toy or kind of toy seems to cause the most problems, contact the toy manufacturer, your legislators, or your state attorney general's office. Seek their advice.

▷ Write a letter to the editor of your local newspaper, describing the problem and what you have learned.

▷ Pass a petition asking that the problem be corrected (see pages 153–154). Present your petition to legislators and officials at the attorney general's office.

■ Start a safety club.

▷ Research and practice the best ways to stay safe at home, at school, and in the community.

▷ Focus on everyday safety issues—walking alone, biking, strangers, sports (football, biking, skating).

▷ Have special meetings on what to do in case of fires, accidents, emergencies, and disasters.

■ Organize a first-aid training session for your classroom, school, club, or community group.

▷ Contact your local scout troop, hospital, or Red Cross to ask for someone qualified to do the training.

▷ Be sure to include CPR training in your course.

▷ Teach simple first-aid skills to younger children.

■ Conduct a natural disaster awareness campaign.

▷ Learn about a natural disaster that is a special problem in your part of the country (earthquake, flood, forest fire, tornado, etc.).

▷ Learn what to do when disaster strikes.

▷ Give speeches to other classes, schools, clubs, religious organizations, and community agencies on what you have learned.

■ Raise money to buy smoke detectors for all the homes in your neighborhood or for your school, club, or church (see pages 167–169).

■ Make emergency kits for your home, school, club, etc. You might include:

▷ bottled water

▷ boxed juice

▷ canned food

▷ packaged food

▷ munchies (nuts, raisins, trail mix, etc.)

▷ matches and candles

▷ string

▷ a solar blanket

▷ a flashlight

▷ extra batteries

▷ a first-aid kit

▷ a first-aid instruction card

▷ a portable radio

▷ medicines

▷ a big sheet of plastic

▷ water purification tablets

▷ garbage sacks

▷ needles and thread

▷ tools (can opener, scissors, knife, screw driver, etc.)

▷ extra clothing and shoes

▷ personal items (comb, toothbrush, toothpaste, deodorant, etc.)

▷ rope

▷ moistened towelettes.

■ Interview firefighters, police officers, rescue squad personnel, and other people who deal with emergencies as part of their job.

▷ Find out what their jobs are like.

▷ Ask them how they handle safety issues.

> ▷ Write an article for your school, neighborhood, community, or city newspaper about what you learned during the interviews.

■ Contact your state legislators. Work for a resolution to set aside one day each year for businesses to train their employees on what to do in a disaster (see pages 159–160).

■ Contact your legislators and ask them to sponsor a law requiring seatbelts in school buses (see pages 163–164).

■ Create a motorcycle safety awareness campaign.
> ▷ Make fliers and posters to hand out and post.
> ▷ Give speeches on motorcycle safety.
> ▷ Invite experts to speak to your community on motorcycle safety.

■ Create a flier for younger kids on any safety topic that interests you (see pages 152–153). Examples: bicycle safety, seatbelts, walking, strangers, playground safety, lightning, skateboards, skates, swimming, guns, fire prevention, household accidents, etc.

■ Give a speech on the importance of wearing helmets when biking, skating, or skateboarding.

■ Write a safety play about any subject that interests you (bicycles, skateboards, swimming, fire, poison prevention, guns, etc.)
> ▷ Present it at schools, clubs, community centers, and religious organizations.
> ▷ Videotape your play. Make copies for libraries.

■ Write a rap song for a public service announcement (PSA) on a safety issue (see pages 158–159).
> ▷ Contact radio stations to request air time.

■ Write letters to the editors of local newspapers on a specific safety issue.

■ Go on a radio talk show to discuss gun safety or another safety issue. Research your topic thoroughly so you'll be prepared to answer questions.

■ Organize a Safe Walking Service to escort young children to and from schools.

■ Inspect your school playground for hazards. Remove or repair them.

■ Write a proposal for a sports safety clinic at your school (see page 157).

   ▷ Present your proposal to the faculty and administration.

   ▷ Invite experts on sports safety to speak at your school.

■ Write a proposal for a self-defense class at your school, club, or religious organization.

More Ideas for Promoting Safety in Your Community

- Write a proclamation about a safety goal to hang in your school (see pages 155–156).

    ▷ Or write a proclamation commending an individual or group who has helped to make your community a safer place.

- Are students allowed to participate in local safety boards or councils? If not, petition for student positions (see pages 153–154).

- Start a Safe Baby-Sitting Club.

    ▷ Recruit baby-sitters for your club.

    ▷ Make it a requirement for every baby-sitter to take the American Red Cross baby-sitting class. Contact your local American Red Cross chapter to find out where and when this class is offered.

▷ Advertise your Safe Baby-Sitting Club on posters and fliers around your neighborhood. Describe the special training club members have had. Include a contact person and telephone number. The contact person will match baby-sitters with families who call in.

▷ Create a baby-sitter's safety guide and distribute it to all club members.

▷ Make cards for every member listing emergency telephone numbers and safe baby-sitting tips. They should bring the card to every baby-sitting job.

■ Make Halloween safety kits for younger children. You might include:

▷ a flier of Halloween safety tips (see pages 152–153)

▷ a flashlight

▷ a bag for carrying treats

▷ a toothbrush and toothpaste.

■ Create a video on holiday safety tips (Halloween, Fourth of July, Memorial Day, Labor Day, New Year's Eve, Christmas, Hanukkah, etc.).

▷ Show it over your school video system.

▷ Show it at other schools, clubs, religious organizations, and community centers.

■ Start a campaign against teen suicide.

▷ Hold a panel discussion on preventing teen suicide.

▷ Make fliers about teen suicide prevention (see pages 152–153). Distribute your fliers to schools, clubs, religious organizations, and community centers.

▷ If your community doesn't offer a teen suicide prevention hotline, start one. Find a community agency that will accept the calls, then advertise the number in your community.

■ Seek training as an EMT (Emergency Medical Technician).

▷ Contact your local fire department or Red Cross office to ask where to go for training. (There might be an age minimum in your state.)

▷ Volunteer for your local EMT team or for an ambulance service. They might find ways for you to help out even if you aren't trained as an EMT.

■ Volunteer at your local fire station or police station. Ask what you can do to help.

■ Volunteer to work at a swimming pool or other public swimming place (lake, pond). Keep watch over the swimmers or help out in other ways.

■ Write a car safety checklist. You might include tips on:

▷ keeping the car in good repair

▷ winterizing

▷ wearing seatbelts

▷ following the recommended maintenance schedule.

■ Create a checklist on what to do if you are stranded in a car. Distribute copies of your checklist.

■ Hold a panel discussion on the dangers of drinking and driving. Invite experts to talk to your group.

■ Hold alcohol-free parties. Attend alcohol-free parties.

▷ Provide designated drivers for teenagers after parties where alcohol is served.

Start a Poison Control Awareness Campaign

In 1992, 1,864,188 poisonings were reported to poison control centers in the United States. 1,092,568 were children under six years old. Adults can forget how quickly and easily children get into things. When you make children more aware of poisons, you're helping the parents and saving the kids.

1. Contact your local Poison Control office. Look for the number in the front of your telephone book under "Emergency Numbers," or dial "0" and ask the operator for the number.

■ Ask for information about poisonings in your state or community.

■ Ask about the poisons commonly found in most homes.

2. Make a flier for kids on poison awareness (see pages 152–153). Be sure to include:

■ the phone number of the local Poison Control Center

■ tips on what to tell Poison Control when you call (see the box below)

■ a list of the most common ways in which kids are poisoned

■ a list of common household poisons to avoid.

What To Tell Poison Control When You Call

■ your name

■ your phone number

■ your address

■ the name of the poison (have the bottle, can, jar, or package in front of you)

■ the amount that was taken (if you know)

■ when and where it happened

■ where the person is right now

■ how the person is doing.

3.   Make a flier for parents on how to store poisons safely in the home (see pages 152–153).

■ Go from room to room, listing poisons commonly found in those rooms and describing how to store them safely. Be sure to cover the kitchen, bathroom(s), bedroom(s), laundry area, garage, basement, and attic.

4.   As part of your awareness campaign, write a play to present the information you have learned.

Find Out More

For information on how to promote safety and prevent accidents, write or call:

National Safety Council
Community Safety Programs Area
1121 Spring Lake Drive
Itasca, IL 60143-3201
(708) 285-1121

SENIOR CITIZENS

Lend a Hand to Your Senior Friends

Many senior citizens live alone, with no family members nearby. Many have a hard time getting around. Because many are on fixed incomes, they often can't keep up with increases in the cost of living. They might need a hand—your hand—to make repairs, do maintenance tasks, run errands, or carry groceries.

1. **Find senior friends to help.**

- Look around your neighborhood and faith community.
- Check high-rises, hospitals, and nursing homes.
- Visit your local senior citizens' center.

2. **Ask how you can help them. They might need you to:**

- go shopping with them
- carry their groceries
- go shopping for them
- pick up medicines at the drug store
- do yard work

- rake leaves in the fall
- shovel walks in the winter
- make minor repairs
- take care of their pets
- help with housework
- do painting

- put up shelves
- help them to write letters
- help them to write checks
- help them with budgeting
- help them to arrange for transportation.

Help Seniors Feel More Secure

1.   Survey your neighborhood or another neighborhood in your community to find out which senior citizens don't have deadbolt locks on their doors or smoke alarms in their homes (see pages 161–162).

2.   Ask if they would like your help obtaining locks or smoke alarms.

- Make a list of the senior citizens who want your help. Then you will know how many locks or alarms you will need.

3.   Ask for donations of the locks or alarms.

■ Or fundraise for money to purchase the items yourself (see pages 167–169).

4.   Call your local police department.

■ Ask if they will help you to install the locks or alarms.

5.   Arrange to speak before your local community council. Ask for community support in helping senior citizens to feel more secure.

Be a Friend

■ Sing to seniors, perform a play, give a magic show, or play a musical instrument. (What's your special talent?)

■ Keep them company.
  ▷ Listen to them. Talk to them. Read to them.

■ Write down their personal histories.
  ▷ Type them into a word processor.
  ▷ Print them out, put them in a special folder, and give them to the seniors.

■ Take them for walks. (Check with the administrator first.)

■ Visit them regularly.

More Ideas for Helping Senior Citizens

■ Work for legislation designed to help senior citizens (see pages 163–164 and 166–167). You might choose to work on one or more of these issues:

▷ health care for seniors

▷ medical benefits

▷ entertainment facilities

▷ improved housing

▷ transportation

▷ accessibility of public buildings, apartment buildings, etc.

▷ eye screening

▷ educational opportunities

▷ nutrition.

■ Does your community offer Meals-on-Wheels for senior citizens?

▷ If it does, volunteer to help.

▷ If it doesn't, work with city officials to start a service that delivers meals to seniors.

- Register seniors to vote (see pages 116–117).

- Help them to acquire mail-in ballots if they are unable to go to the polling place.

- Work for senior representation on local boards and councils.

- Teach your senior friends how to use computers.

Find Out More

To learn more ideas for helping senior citizens, contact your local senior citizens' service groups. Or write or call:

National Council for Senior Citizens
1331 F Street, NW
Washington, DC 20004
(202) 347-8800

TRANSPORTATION

Work to Improve Transportation

Are there people in your school or community who are in need of transportation? Are there others you can convince to carpool? Do some people need encouragement to walk? Do others need to be protected? Moving around town can present problems for some people. Can you think of a need involving transportation in your area—and a solution?

■ Survey your neighborhood to find out how many people are willing to carpool (see pages 161–162).

   ▷ If you get to school by car, organize a carpool.

   ▷ Encourage adults to carpool to and from work.

■ Provide transportation services for senior citizens or people with special needs.

■ Organize a safe walking system to escort young children around the neighborhood or to and from school.

■ Initiate a city ordinance or state law to lower bus fares for youths (see pages 163–164).

■ Start a hotline for any young person who needs transportation. Your hotline might help:

> ▷ teenagers who need rides home from parties where alcohol is being served

> ▷ teenagers who need designated drivers for prom night

> ▷ baby-sitters who need rides home because the parents have been drinking

> ▷ kids who have missed the bus home from school

> ▷ young people who take the wrong bus and get lost

> ▷ teenagers who have car trouble.

■ Start a campaign to bike, walk, or bus to school instead of riding in cars.

■ Fundraise for additional bike racks at school (see pages 167–169).

■ Hold a walk-a-thon or bike-a-thon to raise money for transportation projects.

■ Get involved in influencing the future of your city's transportation system. You might work for (or against):

> ▷ increased bus service

> ▷ a light-rail or monorail system

> ▷ more commuter trains.

More Ideas for Improving Transportation

■ Adopt a pothole. Raise funds to repair it (see pages 167–169).

■ Adopt part of a local highway. Work with friends, classmates, or your club to clean up the litter once a month.

■ Plant native flowers or plants along highways.

■ Adopt a billboard. Use it for a transportation message. Examples: Promote carpooling. Encourage people to walk, bike, or take the bus. Invite people to adopt part of a local highway.

■ Campaign for additional lighting along poorly lighted streets.

■ Campaign for additional crosswalks, cross-overs, and/or street lights.

■ Create your own snow removal company in your neighborhood.

  ▷ Shovel walks, stairs, and driveways for people who can't do it themselves.

■ Distribute leaf bags during the fall. Encourage residents to clean leaves from their streets as well as their yards.

■ Distribute bus schedules at your school, in your neighborhood, and in your community.

■ Make a flier (see pages 152–153) listing and describing the different types of transportation available in your community (buses, carpools, trains, subways, light rail, etc.).

   ▷ Include contact telephone numbers.

   ▷ Make copies of your flier to hand out at school, in your neighborhood, and in your community.

■ Clean up bus stops, bus stations, and subways.

   ▷ Pick up litter.

   ▷ Paint over graffiti.

   ▷ Work with the police to organize a citizen safety watch.

Find Out More

Check your local telephone book for your State Department of Transportation and City Road information numbers. Ask about policies and plans for roads, highways, mass transit, railroads, etc.

Write or call:

   Department of Transportation
   400 Seventh Street, SW
   Washington, DC 20590
   (202) 366-4000
   Provides information on policies for highways, mass transit, railroads, airlines, waterways, oil and gas pipelines, etc.

SERVICE
PROJECT
HOW-TOS

How to Create a Flier

Do you want to hand out information in your school or community? Would you like to make people aware of an issue, tell them about services that are available to them, or share important facts you have learned about a community problem or concern? A one-page flier is a fast and easy way to spread the news.

1. Give it a title.

2. Describe the problem or issue.

3. Describe your project.

4. Include the dates when your project will start and end.

5. Tell readers where your project will take place.

6. Describe yourself, your team, and your sponsor.

7. Will there be a special event? Include the date, place, and times.

8. Tell readers where to write or call for more information.

9. Explain what's in it for them. Prizes? Fun? Fame? The satisfaction of knowing they have made a difference in their community?

10. Include a picture or a cartoon. If possible, use color.

11. For visual interest, vary the sizes of your words.

12. Keep it lively!

How to Create a Petition

Petitions for such things as referendums must follow special instructions. Check with your state office for details. For other petitions, you might follow these steps.

1. Give it a title.

2. Write a statement describing your issue. Put it at the top of *every* page of your petition. That way, people can't say later that they didn't know what they were signing.

3. Leave room for people to write their names *and* their addresses and phone numbers (if they are willing to give that information).

4. For a student petition, leave room for people to write their class, grade, and/or school.

5. Make a copy of your petition. That way, if the original gets lost or destroyed, you still have proof of your petition and the signatures you collected in support of your cause.

How to Create a Press Release

What happens when you send out a press release about your service project to local newspapers, TV stations, and radio stations? Reporters might come...or they might not. But it can't hurt to try. If you do attract media attention to your project, more people will be aware of what you are doing. More people will know about the needs of the person or people you are trying to serve. And more people may decide to get involved, too.

1. Give it a headline.

2. Include the name and telephone number of a contact person.

3. Follow the "five W's." Tell your reader:

- *who* will be involved

- *what* will happen

- *when* it will happen

- *where* it will happen

- and *why* it will happen.

4. Add any details you feel are interesting and important.

5. Keep it short...one page or less!

How to Create a Proclamation

A proclamation is a fancy way to make a public announcement. Mayors, council members, or local government administrators write proclamations to commend people or to announce upcoming events.

1. Contact your mayor's office to request the proclamation.

2. Send a letter to the mayor stating what you would like the proclamation to say.

3. Make an appointment to meet with the mayor for the signing of the proclamation. Usually, the mayor will let you take a photograph of him or her signing the proclamation. You can use the photograph to advertise your project, if you get the mayor's permission first.

Sample Proclamation

WHEREAS,	all students have a right to be safe at school, and
WHEREAS,	fights in the halls are causing problems for everyone, and
WHEREAS,	we all want our school to be a better environment for learning and growing, and
WHEREAS,	we should join together to make our school a safe place to be,
NOW, THEREFORE,	be it resolved that we hereby proclaim October 14 as:

"Fight-Free Friday"

and ask all students to cooperate in keeping the peace.

Signed and sealed this 11th day of October, 19__

_____

Student Body President

_____

Principal

How to Create a Proposal

Do you have a great idea for improving your neighborhood, school, or community? What about starting a hiking club? Making the food in your school lunchroom more nutritious? Describe your idea in a written proposal. Then present your proposal to someone (a teacher, club leader, city official) who has the power to help you make it happen.

1. Give it a title.

2. Name your audience (To: _____).

3. Identify yourself or your group (From: _____). Include your sponsor's name.

4. Write the date on your proposal.

5. Describe the project you are proposing.

6. Describe step-by-step how you plan to carry out your project.

7. List any equipment or services you will need.

8. What will your project cost? Include a budget.

9. Include the dates when your project will start and end.

10. Keep it simple!

How to Create a Public Service Announcement (PSA)

How would you like to broadcast your message over the radio or TV? Every station or channel sets aside a certain amount of free air time for announcements from the public. They are usually 10, 20, or 30 seconds long. The 10-second spots are played most often. Here's how to prepare your PSA.

1.   Give the name and address of your group.

2.   Describe your "target audience"—the people you want to reach.

3.   Specify dates when your PSA should *start* being aired and *stop* being aired. (You don't want it to air after your project is over.)

4.   Include the name and phone number of a contact person.

5.   Briefly state your topic—the purpose of your PSA.

6.   Time your PSA to last for 10, 20, or 30 seconds.

7.   Write "END" at the bottom of your PSA to show that it is finished.

8.   Radio stations will usually accept a taped cassette. Television usually requires professional work. Cable channels might supply this professional help.

■ Contact your local stations and channels for specific requirements.

How to Create a Resolution

A resolution is less binding than a law. It is a strong suggestion for action, supported by your legislators. Here's how to create one.

1.   Contact your state legislator. Explain your idea. Your legislator may offer to work with you.

2.   Make sure that your resolution won't conflict with any existing laws. Check with your legislator.

3.   Follow the form shown on page 160. Resolutions are very formal. Yours will get more attention if you show that you know the rules.

4.   Expect that your resolution will be debated. Some people will argue for it, and some people will argue against it. This is normal for resolutions.

5.   Get local governments involved. Ask that your resolution be presented at local meetings.

6.   You could also create a resolution that doesn't have legislative backing. Follow the form, then present your resolution to your school or community.

Sample Resolution

WHEREAS,	fires, floods, and storms result in many injuries and deaths each year to citizens of our state, and
WHEREAS,	many of these injuries and deaths could be avoided with proper preparation and fast, appropriate response, and
WHEREAS,	the business setting is an excellent environment for training and education, and
WHEREAS,	it is in the best interests of business to teach their employees disaster response skills and techniques; therefore be it
RESOLVED, that	on the first Wednesday of each March, businesses in our state will provide disaster response training for their employees.

SIGNED and DATED this _____ day of January, 19__

_____   _____
Governor   Lieutenant Governor

How to Create a Survey

There are many different types of surveys. For example, an Opinion Survey collects people's opinions about an issue ("Do you think that changing the school starting time from 8:00 to 9:30 is a good idea?"). An Information Survey gathers information you can use to give your issue credibility ("Would you support changing the school's starting time from 8:00 a.m. to 9:30 a.m.? Yes or no?") An Awareness Survey determines whether people are aware of an issue. ("Have you heard that the school board wants to change the school starting time from 8:00 to 9:30?") TIP: Surveys don't usually ask for long answers. When you need long answers, conduct interviews.

■ To create an Opinion Survey:

  ▷ Write a few strong statements (five at the most) about your issue.

  ▷ Ask people if they Strongly Agree, Agree, Disagree, or Strongly Disagree with each statement.

  ▷ Record their answers.

  ▷ Or you can ask simple "Yes" or "No" questions. But you learn more by asking people if they agree or disagree, and how strongly.

■ To create an Information Survey:

  ▷ Write a few strong statements to *explain* the information, or a few questions which *ask* for information.

▷ Ask people if they Support or Don't Support, Agree or Disagree with the ideas in your survey.

▷ Record their answers.

▷ Leave room for them to add suggestions.

▷ Use your own variations on this survey, depending on your issue and the kind of information you want to collect.

■ To create an Awareness Survey:

▷ Write a few strong statements about your issue.

▷ Ask people if they Support or Don't Support, Agree or Disagree with the ideas in your survey.

▷ Record their answers.

▷ Describe any action you suggest.

▷ Explain where to go or what to do if you suggest an action.

▷ Leave room for them to add suggestions.

▷ Use your own variations on this survey, depending on your issue.

■ When you finish your survey, tabulate your findings. Then look at them carefully.

▷ What did you learn from your survey?

▷ Were there any surprises?

■ Decide how you will use your survey results.

▷ Will you place your results on a graph or chart? This makes them easier to see and understand at a glance.

▷ Will you present your results to a group?

▷ Will you share them with an agency or organization that has a connection to your problem?

▷ It's important to share your results. Otherwise there's no point in doing a survey.

How to Initiate an Ordinance or Law

Laws are made by your state legislatures or state houses. Ordinances are laws or rules passed by city officials. You can't actually create a law or ordinance, but you can have an idea for one and try to get adults to create it for you.

1. Choose a problem you think needs solving.

2. Research your problem carefully. Does it seem as if a new ordinance or law would help to solve the problem?

■ Pass a petition to find out if other people support your idea (see pages 153–154.)

3. Contact your mayor, commission, administrator, legislator, or staff person. Explain your idea and ask for support.

4. Your ordinance or law will then be:
   ▷ discussed by lawmakers
   ▷ investigated by a staff person
   ▷ legally reviewed (to make sure it doesn't conflict with existing laws)
   ▷ drafted in legal language

▷ opened for discussion at a public hearing (you can get permission to get on the agenda and testify for your law or ordinance)

▷ signed, not signed, or vetoed (rejected).

How to Lobby

■ Make sure you have researched your topic. You should know it backwards and forwards.

■ If possible, start lobbying *before* the legislative session begins.

▷ You can lobby by phone, by letter, in person, and by testifying before committees.

▷ You can present your issue to an interim committee (a committee which meets between sessions).

■ Find a sponsor.

▷ Look for a legislator who will support your cause and help you through the process.

▷ Find others who are concerned about your issue. Ask them to help.

■ Make one or more posters to bring to committee meetings.

▷ Your posters should present, reinforce, and clarify your idea.

▷ Make them large enough so the whole committee can read them from a distance.

▷ If you present your ideas in legislative chambers, you may not be allowed to bring your posters with you. Check first.

■ Make a one-page flier to give to each lawmaker you lobby. Your flier should include:

▷ your bill number and title, and a brief description of what the bill says

▷ your sponsor's name and title

▷ your reasons for supporting or opposing the bill

▷ your request for support from the lawmakers.

■ Build coalitions of support.

▷ Find other people who agree with you.

▷ Ask them to help you lobby.

How to Start a Statewide Fund

1. Contact a sponsor in your legislature, preferably one who represents your area, and ask for his or her support.

■ Your goal is to see if your legislature will agree to set aside a small portion of taxpayers' money for your fund, *not* to raise new taxes.

2. Create a one-page flier to promote your idea to legislators (see pages 152–153).

3.   Lobby for your fund (see pages 164–165).

▪ Ask for a reasonable amount from your legislature—for example, $5,000–$10,000.

4.   Figure out how to manage and promote your fund.

▪ You might set it up as a series of "matching grants." For example, kids would agree to fundraise or donate $100 for every $100 grant they received from the fund.

▪ The money could be kept in a state administrator's office. The administrator could manage the fund and award the grants.

▪ Or you might ask a state education office to manage the fund.

5.   Make fliers to send out to all schools or districts in your state (see pages 152–153), announcing that the money from the fund is available in grants up to a level you specify. Your fund manager might agree to send out the announcements for you.

How to Support or Oppose a Law

1.   Call your state legislature or state house.

▪ Ask if the legislators are currently considering any bills or measures related to your issue. (A bill or measure is what a piece of legislation is called before it becomes a law.)

■ Ask to be sent a list of bills or measures, including the names of the sponsors.

■ Read the list and decide if there are any bills or measures you want to support or oppose.

2.   Contact the legislators who represent your area. (They might be offended if you don't include them in your project. After all, you are their constituents—the people they represent). Tell your legislators what you are planning. They might give you ideas for additional laws to support or oppose or even initiate a new law for you.

3.   Choose a specific law that you want to support or oppose.

4.   Lobby for your law (see pages 164–165). Try to convince legislators to vote the way you want them to.

Seven Ways to Fundraise

Do you need to raise money to do your project? Here are some ways that have worked for other people.

1.   Perform a service for a fee. Examples:

■ lead tours of your community

■ collect cans, newspapers, etc. for recycling

- rake leaves

- mow lawns

- shovel snow

- wash cars

- walk dogs.

2.   **Sell something. Examples:**

- food (you might need a food handler's license unless you use prepackaged foods such as chocolates or baked goods)

- seasonal or holiday items

- goods such as pencils, paper, socks—anything people need and use

- cards, directories, or coupons.

Cow Pie Bingo

Many high schools around the United States have tried this unusual fundraiser. They section off a football field into squares, sell each square for a dollar, and turn a cow loose on the field. The winner is selected by the cow...guess how!

3.   **Ask for donations. Places to try:**

- your neighborhood

- your community

- your school

- youth groups

- civic groups (Lions, Rotary Club, VFW, etc.).

4.   **Have a special event. Suggestions:**

- rummage sale

- carnival

- contest or game

- auction

- play or performance (or show a film).

5.   **Campaign for officials running for election.** Sometimes they can pay you from campaign funds.

6.   **Try to get a grant.** Ask your principal or check at your library reference desk for organizations that give grants, including:

- educational foundations

- private foundations

- corporations

- the government.

7.   **Get help from a professional fundraiser.** You will have to pay the fundraiser a percentage of the money that is raised. Be sure that you know in advance what this percentage will be. Do you think you can raise enough to fund your project AND pay the fundraiser?

Index

Praise for
The Kid's Guide to Service Projects

"A gold mine for kids who want to make a difference."
—*NEA Today*

"An outstanding choice."
—*School Library Journal*

About the Author

Barbara A. Lewis is a national award-winning author and educator who teaches kids how to think and solve real problems. Her students at Jackson Elementary School in Salt Lake City, Utah, have worked to clean up hazardous waste, improve sidewalks, plant thousands of trees, and fight crime. They have instigated and pushed through several laws in their state legislature and an amendment to a national law, garnering 10 national awards including two President's Environmental Youth Awards, the Arbor Day Award, the Renew America Award, and A Pledge and a Promise Environmental Award. They have also been recognized in the *Congressional Record* three times.

Barbara has been featured in many national newspapers, magazines, and news programs including *Newsweek, The Wall Street Journal, Family Circle, CBS This Morning, CBS World News*, and CNN. She has also written many articles and short stories for national magazines. Her other books for Free Spirit Publishing— *The Kid's Guide to Social Action*, *Kids with Courage*, and *What Do You Stand For?*—have won numerous awards and honors.

Barbara has lived in Indiana, New Jersey, Switzerland, and Belgium. She and her husband, Larry, currently reside in Park City, Utah. They have four children: Mike, Andrea, Chris, and Sam.

Other Great Books by Barbara A. Lewis

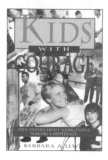